# TRANQUILITY GROVE

## GROVE

### The Great Abolitionist Picnic of 1844

MARTHA REARDON BEWICK

A Hingham Historical Commission Project

AMERICA
THROUGH TIME®
ADDING COLOR TO AMERICAN HISTORY

*Back cover illustration, left*: "This is the Lord's Doing," Garrison's anti-slavery banner, 1843. (*Collection of Massachusetts Historical Society*)

*Back cover illustration, right*: Portrait of John Quincy Adams, William Hudson, Jr., 1844. (*Collection of National Portrait Gallery*)

America Through Time is an imprint of Fonthill Media LLC
www.through-time.com
office@through-time.com

Published by Arcadia Publishing by arrangement with Fonthill Media LLC
For all general information, please contact Arcadia Publishing:
Telephone: 843-853-2070
Fax: 843-853-0044
E-mail: sales@arcadiapublishing.com
For customer service and orders:
Toll-Free 1-888-313-2665

www.arcadiapublishing.com

First published 2018

Typeset in Sabon LT Std
Printed and bound in England

*In honor of Wilmon Whilldin Blackmar (1841–1905), Recipient of the Congressional Medal of Honor in 1897, Hingham benefactor, and Commander-in-Chief of the Grand Army of the Republic; and Hingham's seventy-five sons who gave their lives during the Civil War.*

*and*

*In memory of my parents, Justice Paul Cashman Reardon and Ann Leich Reardon, who loved the history and legends of Massachusetts and of our home communities on the South Shore: Quincy, Plymouth, and Hingham.*

Abolitionist Picnic in Weymouth Landing, Susan Torrey Merritt, 1845.
(*Courtesy of Art Institute of Chicago*)

# Acknowledgments

I was invited to undertake the research leading to this small volume for the Hingham Historical Commission by Alexander Macmillan, Hingham's Town Historian. I am particularly grateful to Alec, and to Andrea Young, Administrator of the Commission, for providing this fascinating assignment, and for their patience as it slowly made its way to publication. Members of the Hingham Historical Commission, who sponsored the investigation, demonstrated continuing interest and enthusiasm for the project, and even walked through the brambles on the property with an eye to restoring the old Grove for the citizens of Hingham and the region. They were joined by former Fire Chief Mark Duff, who grew up as a neighbor of Tranquility Grove, and his wife, Geri Duff, as well as Loni Fournier, Director of the Hingham Conservation Commission, which owns the property. Members of the Commission include: Kevin Burke, Sarah Carolan, Signe McCullough, James Conroy, Elizabeth Dings, and Stephen Dempsey. Former Commission members who also participated include Robert Curley, Stephen Swett, and Huck Handy. The Town of Hingham Tax Write-off Program, managed by Kathy Glenzel of Hingham's Senior Center, provided initial assistance.

During the development of the research, I was invited to give presentations about the emerging story in various locations. I would like to thank Gretchen Condon and the Hingham Senior Center, Ron Frazier and the Braintree Historical Society, the Meadows community and Janna Oddliefson for raising some very useful questions, and, Suzanne Buchanan, Virginia Tay and the Hingham Historical Society, who invited me to deliver the Lincoln Day Address at Old Ship Church in February 2017. This was a great honor. I particularly enjoyed the opportunity to sing an abolitionist song or two.

Sabina Beauchard, Reproductions Coordinator, and her team at the Massachusetts Historical Society collected images from their collection of Abolitionist materials, and expedited the research and release of these documents and images, for which I am very grateful! Peter Drummey, Librarian of MHS, was also very encouraging. The Chicago Art Institute sent permission to use Susan Torrey Merritt's *Anti-Slavery Picnic in Weymouth Landing*, a collage created in 1845. Michael Achille, Registrar of the Hingham Historical Society, provided invaluable assistance and images from the Hingham Historical Society's collection, including access to the original 1844 Tranquility Grove banners. Kate Dickerson, who lived in Tranquility Lodge at 137 Main Street, shared the history of the Thaxter home and the 1844 right of way to the Grove, while James and Rosalie Macella opened their home, the former Roseneath Cottage, for a visit.

Hingham historians, including Stephen Dempsey and James Conroy, were helpful and offered moral support as well. Steve Dempsey wrote *Hingham Through Time* with Alexander Macmillan, has published the first of a series on Hingham's architecture, and shared approaches to digitizing photography. James Conroy, who is busy with his own books, including his excellent *Lincoln's White House: The People's House in Wartime*, took the time to scrutinize the manuscript in an earlier draft and offer valuable editorial improvements and suggestions. Emma Ryan, who graduated from Hingham High School in 2018, interviewed me for her National History Day project, a documentary video on the events of Tranquility Grove, which received special recognition in the 2017 competition. Mary Ann Frye, Michael McPherson, and Mike Weymouth were always happy to answer my publishing and graphics questions and point me in the right directions. Cinda Day provided information about Hingham's sons who died in the Civil War, and led the way to Lucretia Leonard's and the Thaxter sisters' graves in the Hingham Cemetery. Eileen Dumont of Weymouth provided valuable information about Maria Weston Chapman.

Thanks to Kena Longabaugh, Josh Greenland, Jay Slater, and Alan Sutton for bringing it all together in the end, and to my family and friends who listened patiently to the stories, especially my brother Dave Reardon, for his helpful research, and my brother Tom Reardon, for his unfailing humor and hospitality. A special thanks to my niece Jennifer Ritterhouse, professor in U.S. history at George Mason University, author, and specialist in the U.S. South and African-American history, for her very welcome advice. And for John, whose dream that every person on earth be loved as a child of God was my companion, even though he is no longer here to share it. For all those who have helped and on whom I have leaned for ideas or support of any kind, even though I may not have mentioned your name, thank you!

# Contents

Acknowledgments                                                        5

Introduction                                                           9
Slavery and Abolitionists                                              9
The Pic Nic of 1844                                                   12
Tranquility Grove                                                     15

1   Preparations for the Pic Nic in Tranquility Grove                 17

2   The News Accounts in *The Liberator* and *Hingham Patriot*        22
Coverage of the August 1 Celebrations in 1844                         22
Hingham's August 2 Celebration                                        24
From the *Hingham Patriot*                                            33
Hingham's Great Day Remembered                                        35

3   Letters and Songs                                                 37
Diary of John Quincy Adams                                            37
Letter from John Quincy Adams                                         39
Letter from Charles Francis Adams                                     40
Journal of Frederick Douglass                                         40
"Hymn for the 1st of August," Almira Seymour                          41
Songs of the Hutchinson Family Singers                                41
Anti-Slavery Songbook of Jairus Lincoln                               42

4   Anti-Slavery Pic Nic Participants                                 47
Marshal: Jairus Lincoln                                               47
President of the Day: William Lloyd Garrison                          49
Vice-Presidents: Bourne Spooner, Robert Purvis                        50

Opening Prayer: Rev. Mr. Oliver Stearns 52
Letters: John Quincy Adams, Charles Francis Adams 52
The Keynote Address, and Afternoon Speakers 56
Music 62
Committee of Arrangements 64

5 Other Hingham Abolitionists 68
Sydney Howard Gay 68
Rev. Samuel J. May 73
Albert Fearing 74
Maria Weston Chapman 74

6 Groves and Tranquility Grove 76
Groves in History 76
The Alcotts and Tranquility Grove 76
Other Hingham Groves 77
Tranquility Grove 80
Tranquility Grove Since 1844 81

7 Tranquility Lodge and Roseneath Cottage 83
Tranquility Lodge and the Right of Way 83
Roseneath Cottage 86
Susan Barker Willard 87

8 Tranquility Grove Property 89
Tranquility Grove Ownership 89
Burns Memorial Park: Tranquility Grove 90
Reclaiming Tranquility Grove 94

Abolitionist Timeline 97

Appendix 99
Letter from John Quincy Adams (as printed in the *Hingham Patriot*) 99
"Hymn for the 1st of August," Almira Seymour 101
"Get Off the Track," Hutchinson Family Singers 102
"The Universalist Sunday School Pic Nic" 104
Announcement of August 1, 1844 Celebration in Concord 107
Ralph Waldo Emerson Address, August 1, 1844, Concord 107

Bibliography 124

# Introduction

## Slavery and Abolitionists

The Anti-Slavery Pic Nic, which took place in Hingham, Massachusetts, in 1844, and which is described in this small book, was one of the thousands of fairs, picnics, conventions, lectures, rallies, petitions to the legislature and Congress, and protest marches sparked by growing opposition to slavery throughout the United States during the eighteenth and nineteenth centuries.

It would all come to a head twenty years later with the Emancipation Proclamation and the devastation of the Civil War. A half-million Union soldiers would die of combat injury and disease during the war, laying down their lives for the cause of emancipation of slaves and preservation of the Union. Another quarter-million Confederate soldiers would give their lives for the Southern cause.

The enslavement of Africans and Indians began in Massachusetts in the early 1600s, and slave trade flourished through the seventeenth and eighteenth centuries. There were 2.9 million enslaved souls in the United States in the 1840s. The end of slavery in Massachusetts occurred when the opinion written by Massachusetts Supreme Court Chief Justice William Cushing of Scituate in 1783 in the Quock Walker case proclaimed that the practice of slavery was incompatible with the Massachusetts Constitution of 1780:

> And upon this ground our Constitution of Government, by which the people of this Commonwealth have solemnly bound themselves, sets out with declaring that all men are born free and equal—and that every subject is entitled to liberty, and to have it guarded by the laws, as well as life and property—and in short is totally repugnant to the idea of being born slaves. This being the case, I think the idea of slavery is inconsistent with our own conduct and Constitution; and there can be no such thing as perpetual servitude of a rational creature, unless his liberty is forfeited by some criminal conduct or given up by personal consent or contract…

Store Room

27

Store Room.

*Above:* Interior of ship designed to transport slaves, packed like common goods to maximize cargo space.

*Left:* Chief Justice William Cushing of Scituate, of the Massachusetts Supreme Judicial Court, wrote the Quock Walker decision in 1783, bringing an end to slavery in Massachusetts. He was one of the first associate justices appointed to the Supreme Court of the United States by George Washington. He was a descendant of the early Cushing settlers of Hingham. Pastel by James Sharples, 1799. (*Collection of National Portrait Gallery*)

With case law, slavery came to a virtual end in the Commonwealth, even though it would take almost 100 years for the Massachusetts legislature to confirm the end of the practice.

Chief Justice Cushing was descended from the Cushings, among the original Hingham settlers. Coincidentally, Levi Lincoln—the Worcester-based attorney for the enslaved Quock Walker, who successfully sued for his freedom—was also descended from original Hingham settlers, the Lincolns, as was Abraham Lincoln. Cushing would later be appointed to the Supreme Court of the United States by George Washington, and, briefly, its Chief Justice. Lincoln would become the 13th Governor of the Commonwealth of Massachusetts in 1825, and later be elected to Congress in 1834.

The earliest anti-slavery abolitionists were Quakers of Pennsylvania, who protested slavery in the seventeenth century. For two centuries, Quakers continued their battle. The Quakers in New Bedford, Massachusetts, were early to provide shelter to escaping slaves. New Bedford became an important refuge to those escaping bondage, including perhaps the most famous, Frederick Douglass.

Boston's greatest anti-slavery efforts and organization were spearheaded by William Lloyd Garrison, who founded *The Liberator* in 1831, the most influential abolitionist newspaper in the United States, as well as the American Anti-Slavery Society in 1833. Douglass wrote about the impact of his first encounter with *The Liberator*:

> ... from this time I was brought into contact with the mind of Mr. Garrison, and his paper took a place in my heart second only to the Bible. It detested slavery, and made no truce with the traffickers in the bodies and souls of men. It preached human brotherhood; it exposed hypocrisy and wickedness in high places; it denounced oppression, and with all the solemnity of "Thus saith the Lord," demanded the complete emancipation of my race. I loved this paper and its editor.

Within five years, the Society would include 1,350 chapters and more than 250,000 members. Women established anti-slavery societies in local communities during the 1830s. For abolitionists, the ending of slavery in the United States was their life's key battle. Some fought on the battlefronts of temperance and women's rights as well. They published anti-slavery newspapers in major cities, lobbied Congress and worked to change state and national laws, organized anti-slavery societies, sponsored fairs, picnics, and lecture tours, and were key organizers of the Underground Railroad, helping fugitives to escape slavery. They wanted "emancipation now."

The Anti-Slavery Pic Nic, which took place in Tranquility Grove in Hingham on August 2, 1844, was just one of these events. Yet the broad and detailed coverage in advertisements and news and journal accounts offers a unique opportunity to witness an important moment in time more than 150 years later.

Today, Emancipation Day is still celebrated in many Caribbean nations on August 1. Juneteenth is celebrated in the United States, marking the emancipation of slaves in Texas on June 19 in 1865.

## The Pic Nic of 1844

On August 2, 1844, an event described as the largest anti-slavery picnic ever held in the United States took place in Hingham, Massachusetts, at what was then known as Tranquility Grove, or Tranquillity Grove. The "Pic Nic," as it was then spelled, celebrated the tenth anniversary of West India Emancipation in 1834, when 800,000 slaves in the West Indies were freed by action of the British Parliament. A reported 6,000–10,000 abolitionists and participants from Norfolk and Plymouth, Suffolk, Middlesex, and Essex counties, ranging from Gloucester through Dedham and Boston to Plymouth, traveled to Hingham for the event by coaches, carriages, and steamboats. One town alone was said to have sent eighty coaches full of participants. Abolitionist speakers and musicians came from throughout the Northeast.

The proposal for an anti-slavery Pic Nic to celebrate the West India emancipation was first suggested by John A. Collins, an abolitionist and student at Andover Theological Seminary, in *The Liberator* on June 24, 1842. Collins published a pamphlet full of suggestions about how to organize such an event. The Reverend Samuel J. May, then the pastor of a church in South Scituate (Norwell), endorsed the suggestion in the same issue of *The Liberator*, saying: "We must have music—joyful noises, shouts, and long and loud huzzas [to present] the story of the First of August ... to the eyes [and] ears of the people." Meanwhile, Sydney Howard Gay, a Hingham-born abolitionist and eventual editor of the *National Anti-Slavery Standard* in New York, a sister journal to *The Liberator*, who had grown up near Tranquility Grove, suggested it as a venue for the great occasion.

These were all Garrisonians, followers of the radical abolitionist William Lloyd Garrison of Boston. May was also the brother of Abigail May Alcott, who had spent happy days in Tranquility Grove when visiting friends in Hingham in 1828. This was during her courtship with educator and transcendentalist Bronson Alcott.

To the abolitionists, celebrating the anniversary of the end of slavery in the British Empire was to become the important patriotic event of the year. Many turned their backs on Fourth of July celebrations, since they believed that the U.S. Constitution supported and condoned slavery. Frederick Douglass, who fled from slavery in 1838, had harsh words about the Fourth of July in a speech given in Rochester, New York, in 1852:

> What to the American slave is your Fourth of July?... To him, your celebration is a sham; your boasted liberty, an unholy license; your national greatness, swelling vanity; your sounds of rejoicing are empty and heartless; your denunciations of tyrants, brass-fronted impudence; your shouts of liberty and equality, hollow mockery; your prayers and hymns, your sermons and thanksgivings, with all your religious parade and solemnity, are to him mere bombast, fraud, deception, impiety and hypocrisy—a thin veil to cover up crimes which would disgrace a nation of savages. There is not a nation on earth guilty of practices more shocking and bloody, than are the people of these United States, at this very hour.

The radical faction, spearheaded by Garrison, called for disunion, or separation from a nation and institutions—even banks, colleges, and churches—that tolerated slavery.

"To the friends of Negro Emancipation," reads the print's inscription. "A glorious and happy era on the first of August, bursts upon the Western World; England strikes the manacle from the slave, and bids the bound go free." Painting, Alexander Rippingille. Engraved by David Lucas (London, 1834).

Those who turned their backs on traditional institutions, radical abolitionists, were called "come-outers." The group who gathered around Garrison, and whose influence reached to the anti-slavery newspapers of New York and Pennsylvania and beyond, became known as "the Boston clique."

In 1844, several August 1 celebrations were scheduled in Massachusetts. There was to be one in Concord and in Hingham, as well as a procession in Fall River, and a parade and lecture in Boston. At the time of the Pic Nic in 1844, Samuel May was in Concord for its widely publicized August 1 celebrations, where Ralph Waldo Emerson was the keynote speaker.

Hingham's August 1 celebration, scheduled outdoors in Tranquility Grove, had to be postponed one day because of rain. Concord's still took place, although the participants were turned away from church venues and eventually found shelter in the Court House. Ralph Waldo Emerson's lengthy and important oration, a chronicle of the horrors of slavery, became the principal speech remembered from that day. (See Appendix.)

The events of August 2 in Hingham included elaborate processions, banners, tables of food prepared by the local committee and brought from Boston, as well as speeches, prayers, and singing. Gathered for the day were well-known individuals representing the heart of the abolitionist movement, both black and white, including participants from Boston and New England, New York and Pennsylvania—outstanding preachers and orators. The Hutchinson Family Singers, the most famous singing group of the day,

Ralph Waldo Emerson.
(*Collection of Massachusetts Historical Society*)

comparable to protest singers of the 1960s such as Peter, Paul, and Mary, Joan Baez, Bob Dylan, or Pete Seeger, sang their anti-slavery anthems and led the throngs in song.

Former President John Quincy Adams, at the time a congressman representing Hingham, sent a long impassioned letter that outlined the complex issues related to the battle against slavery, and set the tone of the day. Speakers included William Lloyd Garrison, Edmund Quincy, Frederick Douglass, and Wendell Phillips, among other luminaries. The year 1844 was also a presidential election year. The election, opposition to the admission of new slave states, and a gag rule barring discussion of slavery in Congress were among the matters of concern that day.

In a memorable conclusion to an already memorable day, the many hundreds of participants from Suffolk, Middlesex, and Essex counties who had come to Hingham by steamboat from Liverpool Wharf in Boston, and who re-boarded the steamboat back to Boston at dusk were marooned on a sandbar, most likely in Hingham Harbor, when the captain misread the tides. As recorded in the journals of John Wallace Hutchinson, one of the family of singers, those aboard endured an uncomfortable night crowded onto the *Portland* with no food or facilities. Frederick Douglass and several of his colleagues spent the night passing resolutions and being calmed by Garrison, who urged them to maintain their dignity. The steamboat with its weary passengers arrived back safely in Boston on the morning tide, in time for breakfast.

## Tranquility Grove

Tranquility Grove was owned by Henry and Edward Thaxter, brothers who lived next door to each other on Hingham's Main Street. Located in an area now bounded by Central, Elm, Emerald, and Hersey Streets in Hingham, the grove had been a popular natural retreat for townspeople for many years.

On the day of the tenth anniversary Celebration of West India Emancipation, an elaborate procession of individuals walking four abreast, including participants carrying banners, girls in white carrying arches of oak leaves, and marching bands, approached Tranquility Grove by a road next to Henry Thaxter's home. At the end of the long day, after the thousands had departed, leaving debris and damage behind, the Thaxters were said to have declared that that was the end of large public gatherings at Tranquility Grove. Shortly thereafter, trees were cut in the grove, and church congregations that had loved to picnic in the grove had to look for new locations.

Ownership of the property has passed through several families since the Thaxters' time. Today, Burns Memorial Park, a green space of 24.1 acres, overgrown with brambles, accessible to the public, owned by the Town of Hingham, and managed by the Hingham Conservation Commission, is what remains of Tranquility Grove. The Town of Hingham is once again looking at this property with the question of how to make it once again attractive to the public. How can the Town best share the story of Tranquility Grove and make the great abolitionist Pic Nic known more widely?

The Pic Nic was an extraordinary gathering, comparable in intensity, organization, message, color, passion and music, and gentle chaos to today's marches on Washington. With the ever-growing opposition to slavery, leading some twenty years later to the Emancipation Proclamation, Hingham's gathering had enduring significance. August 1 celebrations were conducted with deliberate formality, dignity, and decorum, for the most part, so the public could not find grounds for criticism.

In addition to the Pic Nic, Hingham contributed many key figures and memorable moments to the effort to end slavery. This is part of the Town of Hingham's story, and part of the legend of Tranquility Grove.

# I

# Preparations for the Pic Nic in Tranquility Grove

In July 1844, announcements began to appear in the *Hingham Patriot*, *The Liberator*, and in other journals describing the plans for a tenth anniversary Celebration of West India Emancipation in Hingham. One of these declared: "In this Celebration all are respectfully invited to join. It is a day which gave freedom to 800,000 human beings, a day in which all lovers of liberty can unite; a day in which all differences of opinion may be laid aside, and sect and party be forgotten."

Although the British Parliament had ended slavery for 800,000 men, women, and children in the West Indies in 1833, this was not announced to the African slaves on the Caribbean Islands until August 1, 1834. This date, August 1, become a rallying focus for abolitionists in the United States, who were working to end slavery in the United States in town halls, churches, the State House, Congress, and elections.

In Boston, the Massachusetts Anti-Slavery Society was particularly active in organizing abolitionist activities. The Boston group, founded and inspired by William Lloyd Garrison, published anti-slavery newspapers, and, as mentioned, worked with local anti-slavery groups to run fairs, picnics, and lectures supporting their efforts. Celebrations of West India Emancipation Day had become popular in 1842. The Hingham and Plymouth County Anti-Slavery Societies were quick to step up to help organize these events.

Speakers announced for Hingham's Pic Nic were to include William Lloyd Garrison, Wendell Phillips, and Charles Remond among others. The newspaper also reported: "It is expected the Hutchinsons [the famous family singing group] will be present to give additional interest to the meeting."

Jairus Lincoln of Hingham was appointed "Chief Marshal" of the day. Active in town politics and education, he had published *Anti-Slavery Melodies: For the Friends of Freedom* in 1843, a collection of songs written by well-known poets and abolitionists for the Hingham Anti-Slavery Society. The songs included familiar patriotic melodies with militant lyrics against slavery and a country that would tolerate it. The songbook was prepared for use on August 1, 1844.

Lincoln worked with a local Committee of Arrangements, including Hingham residents Gorham Lincoln, John Cushing, Mrs. Edward Lincoln, Miss Anna Quincy

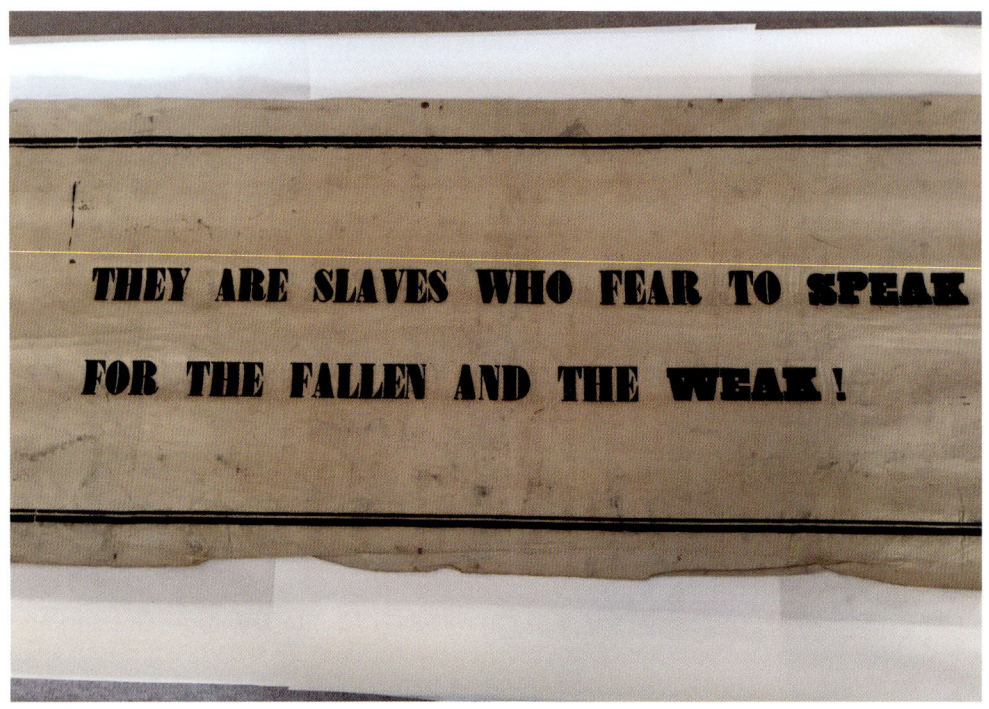

"They are Slaves who fear to speak/For the fallen and the weak!" One of the original banners hung amid the oaks in Tranquility Grove for the celebration of August 2, 1844. (*Collection of Hingham Historical Society*)

Thaxter, and Miss Louise Beal. The committee members were all to be in the Grove for the Pic Nic, to receive the many contributions of refreshments, "to prepare a collation," or a light meal, and to lay them out before the arrival of the expected throngs to the Grove. Others contributing refreshments were invited to bring them to the home of Miss Eliza Thaxter, Anna Quincy Thaxter's sister, on the afternoon before the picnic.

An article written by Marian Studley described the Tranquility Grove collation in more detail. She described "a quantity of supplies," which had been delivered. This included "bread of all kinds, cakes, pies, tea, coffee, cream, lemons, sugar, boiled ham, neats' tongues, fowls, fruits of all sorts, raisins, fresh vegetables, and flowers." These must have come from the Hingham area alone, since she added: "More will come from the office at No. 21 Cornhill Street with the friends from Boston…"

Newspaper announcements advised that those coming from Norfolk and Plymouth counties should gather in designated places in their towns and proceed to a point opposite Rev. Oliver Stearns's Third Congregational Meeting House (New North Church) in Fountain Square. It was there the procession would form.

They were then to proceed to the steamboat landing to meet and welcome those coming from Suffolk, Middlesex, and Essex counties across Boston Harbor. The delegates from Norfolk and Plymouth counties walked from Fountain Square towards

Fountain Square today, with the Third Congregational Church (New North Church), and a statue of Abraham Lincoln, whose Lincoln ancestors lived nearby. Jairus Lincoln and Levi Lincoln were also descendants of the original Lincoln settlers in Hingham.

19

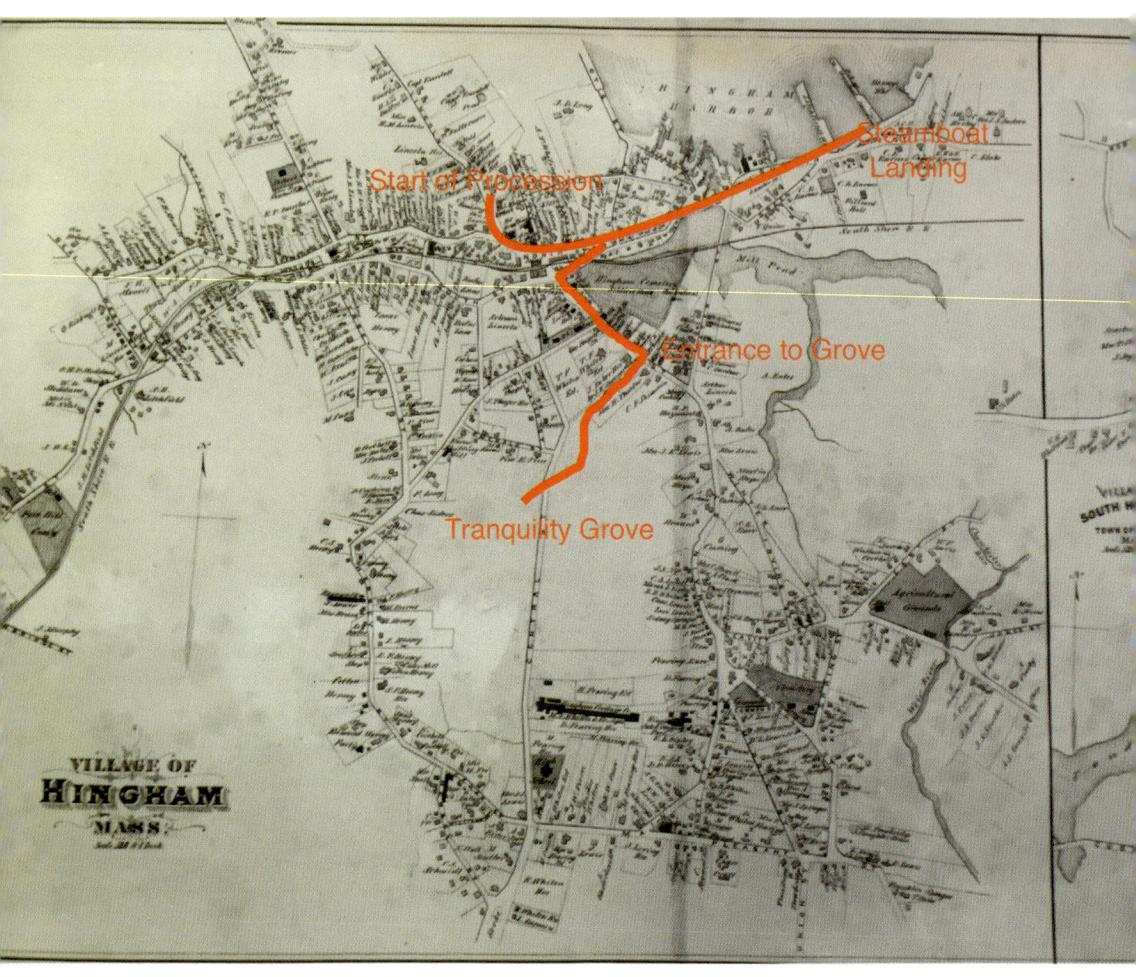

Map of procession route from Fountain Square to the Steamboat Wharf to Tranquility Grove.

the steamboat landing, then lined the route, where they welcomed the delegates from Suffolk and Essex counties, as described in *The Liberator.*

The map showing the procession route postdates 1844. At the time of the great event, Hingham's Elm Street, Emerald Street, and Central Street had not yet been laid out.

The order of procession outlined in the July 26 newspaper announcement was straightforward. Banners for each section came first, followed by the chief of each delegation accompanied by aides, and then followed by the delegation itself. The groups of delegates were interspersed with marching bands.

Order of Procession

Aide   Chief Marshal   Aide

Hingham Banner
Aide   County Marshal   Aide
Plymouth County

Suffolk Banner
Aide   County Marshal   Aide
Music
Norfolk County

The American Anti-Slavery Banner
Music

Suffolk Banner
Aide   County Marshal   Aide
Suffolk County

Essex Banner
Aide   County Marshal   Aide
Essex County

Once the participants arriving by steamboat had joined the procession, the parade of participants, "four abreast," was to proceed from Steamboat Wharf to North Street to South Street to Main Street, and "to enter the Grove at the house of Henry Thaxter, Esq." The right of way led between the Thaxter homes and up the hill and over into the grove, and so the many thousands gathered in Tranquility Grove on August 2, 1844.

# 2

# The News Accounts in
## *The Liberator* and *Hingham Patriot*

William Lloyd Garrison's anti-slavery newspaper, *The Liberator*, carried the most extensive account of the August 1 celebrations in its edition of August 9, 1844. The Annual Report of the Massachusetts Anti-Slavery Society also summarized the August 1 events with enthusiasm: "The illustrious Anniversary of West Indian Emancipation was celebrated in this State with even unusual demonstrations of festivity and temperate joy."

Hingham's local journal, the *Hingham Patriot*, printed its account on August 16, after complaining in its August 9 edition that it had not received an account of the celebration.

## Coverage of the August 1 Celebrations in 1844

Under the title, "The Jubilee—Glorious Demonstration," the various August 1 celebrations in New Bedford, Boston, Concord, and Hingham were described in *The Liberator*. New Bedford's festivities, as Hingham's, had to be postponed one day because of rain. In Concord, August 1 participants sought shelter from the rain, but "to the disgrace of the town" no religious meetinghouse opened its doors to the gathering: "… the doors of every church in the town were barred to the advocates of universal emancipation, and they were compelled to resort to the court-house."

The *Liberator* roundly castigated the Concord "of revolutionary renown," and said that "Its ancient patriotism has utterly perished; and as for its piety, to what shall it be compared but to that which they of old exhibited, who vociferously preferred Barabbas to Jesus?"

Ralph Waldo Emerson's oration, an "address of singular beauty and eloquence," was delivered in Concord's Court House. The address, which can be found in the appendix of this book, was immediately published and widely circulated. The Massachusetts Anti-Slavery Society annual report added that there was "an entertainment," after which "addresses were made by Messrs. W. A. White, S. J. May, Douglass, Cyrus Pierce and others." The others who spoke in Concord, including Frederick Douglass and Rev. Samuel J. May, were forgotten in the wake of Emerson's powerful words, which are still most cited and remembered today.

Boston's August 1 celebration was led by the "Colored Citizens of Boston," in a dignified procession of 300, carrying "appropriate banners," which led to the Tremont Temple. *The Liberator*'s announcement before the celebration described the order of the day:

> Meeting at the Baptist meeting-house in Belknap-street at 1 o'clock. A procession will be formed, and pass through Cambridge, Charles, Beacon and Park streets, to the Tremont Chapel, where addresses will be delivered by several gentlemen who are engaged for the occasion. Friends of the cause in the city and country are invited to be present.

According to the Annual Report of the Massachusetts Anti-Slavery Society, the participants listened to "able and pertinent addresses from Messrs. Roberts and Smith." This was followed by a soiree at 8 p.m., held in the Infant School Room "where an elegant collation was served and the hours pleasantly and profitably filled up by speech and song."

New Bedford's procession and celebration, also postponed until August 2 because of weather, was described in *The Liberator* in some detail describing banners and costumes, music, and grove:

The poster for the Anti-Slavery Celebration of the First of August Anniversary of West India Emancipation held in Worcester in 1851 is typical of the broadsides used to publish these celebrations.

The procession was formed at the new town hall, and consisted of the various benevolent (colored) societies of which there are many in this place, each society dressed uniformly alike, and each bearing its appropriate banner ... escorted by a cavalcade handsomely mounted, accompanied by an excellent band of music from Bristol, R. I. They proceeded to a beautiful grove...

A poster from the 1851 celebration of West India Emancipation, which was held in Worcester, illustrates a typical broadside published and posted to advertise these occasions.

## Hingham's August 2 Celebration

Hingham's event marking the tenth anniversary of the Emancipation of the West Indies, the largest of them all, was described with great enthusiasm by *The Liberator*. The attendance was noteworthy: "It has had no parallel among all the anti-slavery gatherings in the United States on the score of numbers—not less than SIX THOUSAND persons being present—the very flower of the abolition army."

This was echoed in the January 1845 report of the 1844 activities of the Massachusetts Anti-Slavery Society, which exclaimed: "A larger number was assembled than had perhaps ever before met together on any Anti-Slavery occasion. The population of the neighboring towns poured itself upon Hingham in numbers unsurpassed even by the gatherings of political parties." It went on: "The town wore a holiday aspect. The streets were decorated with flags and appropriate mottoes. The bells were rung. It was a day of general rejoicing."

*The Liberator* produced a detailed chronicle of all of the events of the day. The delegates from Norfolk and Plymouth counties assembled at designated locations in Weymouth and South Hingham, "and proceeded en masse to the appointed rendezvous, in their carriages, with joyous music and elevated banners." So large was the attendance from Plymouth County that there was no vehicle available "for miles around, at any price." One town was said to have filled eighty coaches with delegates, and another town sixty.

As participants arrived in Fountain Square, the staging area next to Hingham's Third Congregational Church (New North Church), they gathered under their banners, and were sorted into a marching order by counties by the various parade marshals. The Norfolk and Plymouth county delegates then processed towards the steamboat landing, and separated to line each side of North Street and the street leading to the wharf to welcome the delegates arriving from Boston.

Delegates from Suffolk and Middlesex counties had embarked at Liverpool Wharf in Boston, on board "the splendid and spacious steamer *Portland*."

The steamboat next crossed Boston Harbor to East Boston, where the delegates from Essex County joined them. *The Liberator* captured the flavor of the moment in its exuberant descriptions: "Three hearty cheers were exchanged by the two companies, and the vessel proceeded far on her way, ere the happy hundreds could complete the interchange of their gratulations."

Because of the change in day from August 1 to August 2 for the celebration due to rain, steamboat arrangements had to be changed as well. Had the transportation gone

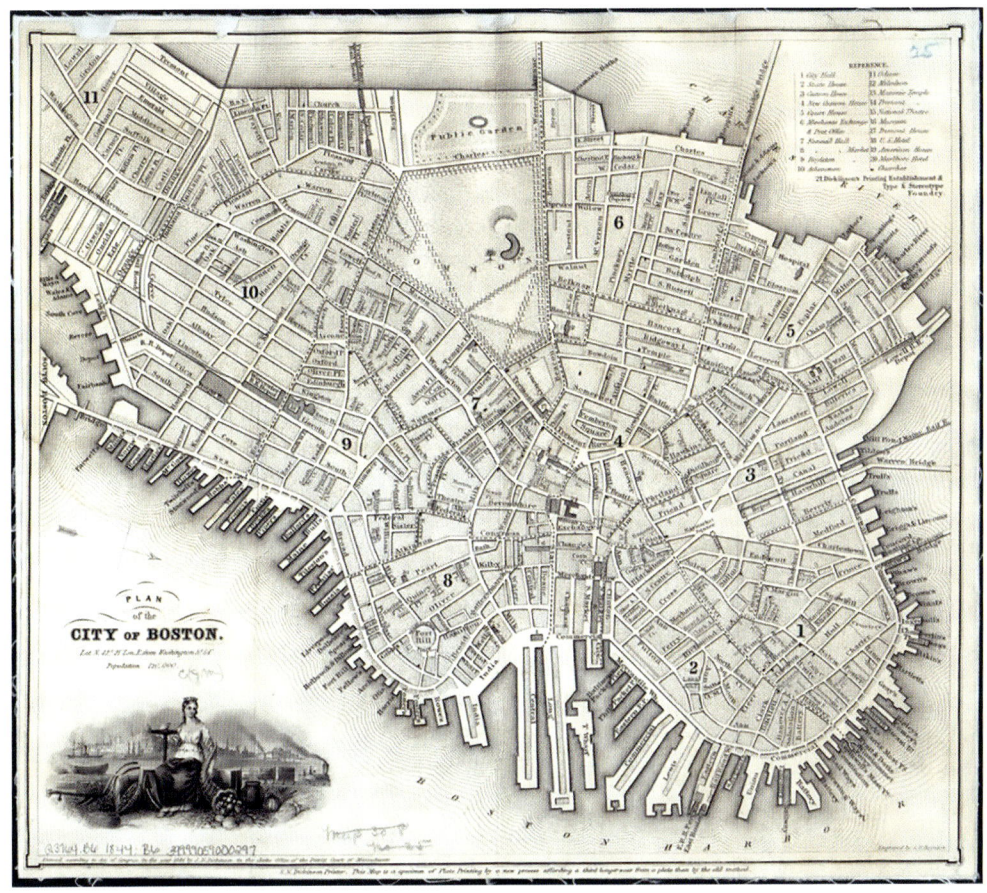

Suffolk and Middlesex county delegates to the 1844 Pic Nic in Hingham boarded the *Portland* at Liverpool Wharf, to the left at the foot of Pearl Street.

according to the original plan, there would have been a smaller steamboat, which would have arrived two hours earlier than the *Portland*. However, the vessel landed safely, and all on board disembarked in Hingham to take their place in the "Grand Procession."

Once the delegates from Suffolk, Essex, and Middlesex counties arrived, the Grand Procession was immediately formed and proceeded along the waterfront to North Street, and down South Street to Main Street to Tranquility Grove. The order of procession was described in detail, led by "the friends of the cause in Hingham preceding the main body as an Escort."

Leading the procession was the chief marshal and his aides on horseback. They were joined by a Legion of Honor, made up of "fifty young ladies, dressed uniformly in white, with wreaths of oak leaves."

Following them came the Hingham Banner, of white silk, bearing on one side the motto, "still achieving—still pursuing," "with a most beautiful and appropriate device, expressing success and aspiration, and on the reverse, 'Hingham Anti-Slavery Society, formed 1835.'"

Next in order in the procession were the Abolitionists of Hingham.

They were followed by the Marshal of Plymouth County, and the Abington Banner, with the motto, "No union with Slaveholders, religiously or politically," and a graphic, "representing the Genius of Freedom shrinking from the offered hand of the slave-driver." The Abington Delegation carried a Banner with the motto "Great is Truth, Great is Liberty, Great is Humanity, and they must and will prevail."

Other towns of Plymouth County walked next, arranged in alphabetical order. The Town of Hanson's Banner had an illustration representing "the Eagle of America trampling a prostrate slave, a bloodhound in the act of seizing the victim, and a file of soldiers pointing their muskets at his body." It also bore the motto, "This is American Liberty," and below that, "Truth shall set you free."

Hanover, and other town delegations from Plymouth County, came into view. The Kingston Banner image was a kneeling slave with the motto, "No union with slaveholders." Another banner read: "Our fanaticism: All men are created equal—thou shall love thy neighbor as thyself."

More Plymouth County delegations walked by, including the Town of Plymouth, with their Banner, representing the landing of the Pilgrims, with the date 1620. Another Plymouth County banner read: "God himself is with us for our Captain."

Essex County's delegation had brought what was described as "the gorgeous Banner of the American Anti-Slavery Society, presented at the late New England Convention." Another banner carried by towns in Essex County, including Lynn and Salem, was "Immediate emancipation the duty of the master, and the right of the slave."

Following Essex County's delegations came the Suffolk County Marshal. He was accompanied by music, Holmes' Boston Band. His banner and illustration were described: "... the hours of emancipation; representing a slave at sunrise on the 1st of Aug. 1834, with the chains falling from his limbs, from which they have just been broken." The banner motto was "This is the Lord's doing. Slavery abolished in the British West Indies, 1st August, 1834."

On came more Boston delegates, carrying a banner with the motto, "The Almighty has no attribute which can take sides with the slaveholder." Then came Chelsea, with a banner of blue silk, inscribed with the word "Chelsea," in gold letters.

Norfolk County was represented by a Marshal, with a Dorchester Banner. Here there were gold letters on an azure field. The illustration was "a slaveholder presenting a deed of emancipation to his chattel personal." Norfolk County's motto read, "Our watchword, Let the oppressed go free." Beneath the illustration were the words, "Be just, and fear not."

Delegations from Dorchester and Norfolk County communities, including Weymouth and Walpole, followed.

The Town of Milton delegation carried a banner illustrated by a Cap of Liberty, and the motto: "God never made a tyrant nor a slave." West Roxbury carried a banner with the motto "He hath sent me To preach deliverance to the captive."

Weymouth and other towns of Norfolk County brought up the end of the procession, also carrying their banners. Delegates from other unnamed counties were at the end of the procession.

*The Liberator* described the appearance of the Procession, as it passed through the principal streets, as "beautiful in the extreme." It reported: "Throughout its entire

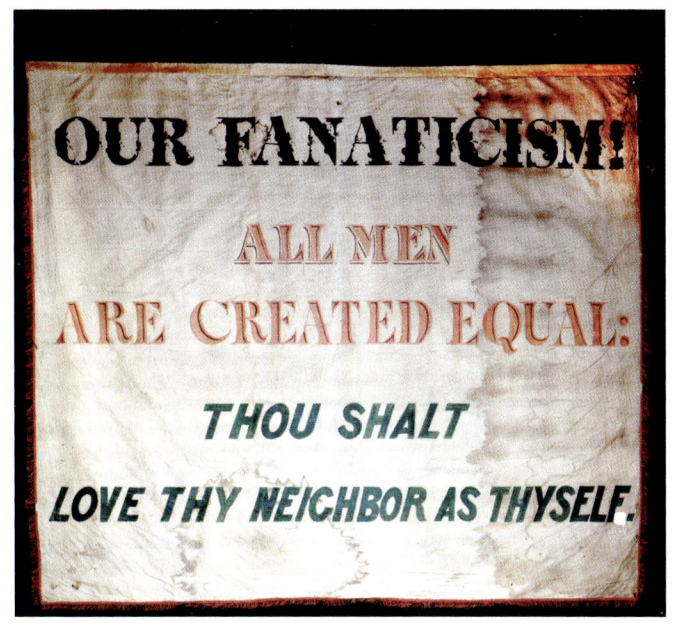

"Our Fanaticism! All Men are Created Equal: Thou Shalt Love Thy Neighbor As Thyself." This banner was carried by the Town of Kingston delegation in the Plymouth County group during the August 1 celebrations in the Town of Hingham in 1844. (*Collection of Massachusetts Historical Society*)

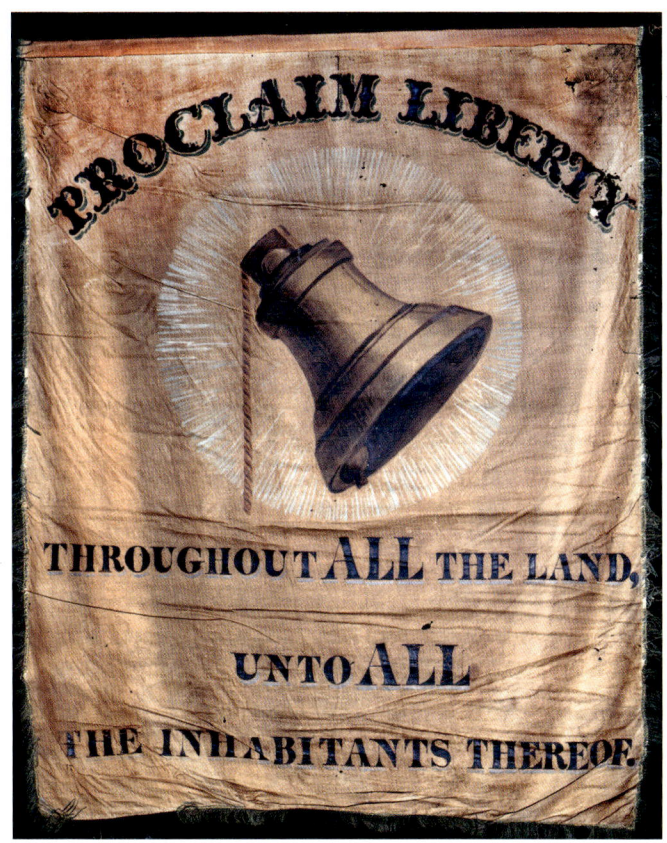

"Proclaim Liberty" was another banner of the kind carried in procession on August 2, 1844 in Hingham. (*Collection of Massachusetts Historical Society*)

"This is the Lord's Doing. Slavery Abolished in the British West Indies. August 1st 1834. Laus Deo." (*Collection of Massachusetts Historical Society*)

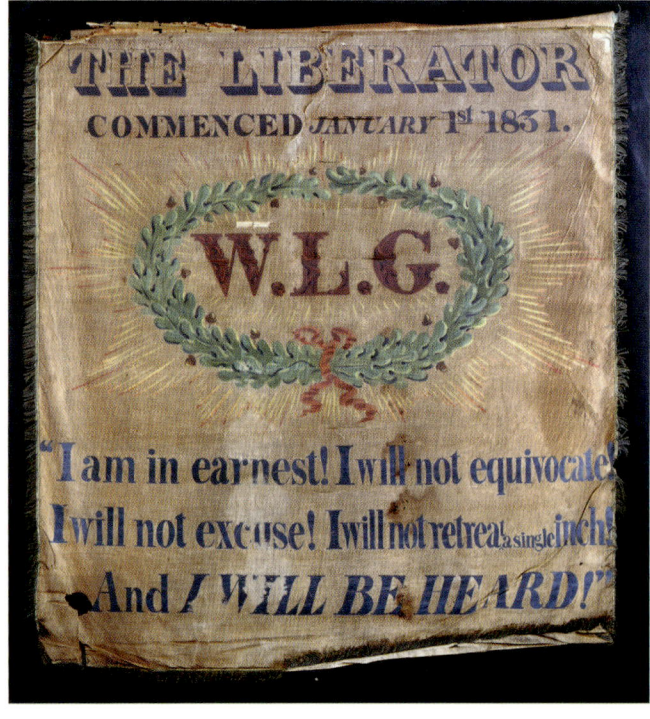

William Lloyd Garrison's original banner, with his great prophetic cry from the first edition of *The Liberator*, January 1, 1831. "I am in earnest! I will not equivocate! I will not excuse! I will not retreat one single inch! And I WILL BE HEARD!" (*Collection of Massachusetts Historical Society*)

length, of nearly a mile and a half, splendid banners were displayed at short intervals, which, with the varied dresses and imposing numbers of its almost countless ranks, attracted universal attention and admiration."

Those marching in the procession walked four abreast, and "young and old, rich and poor, male and female, mingled with harmony and pleasure in the promiscuous files."

Once the procession arrived at Tranquility Grove, the parade divided and countermarched, so that everyone could see the banners and participants from other counties and towns. At that point, all gathered around the speakers' platform, and gave "nine cheers" and took their seats.

The day's proceedings commenced. William Lloyd Garrison was named the Chair and the President of the Day. Bourne Spooner of Plymouth and Robert Purvis of Philadelphia were named Vice-Presidents. The events of the day were opened by a prayer from Rev. Mr. Oliver Stearns of the Third Congregational Church in Hingham (New North Church today); after which, letters were read from John Quincy Adams, who was called "the old man eloquent," and his son, Charles Francis Adams. The first full address of the day was given by Edmund Quincy of Dedham.

After the preliminary proceedings, the newspaper reported, all "adjourned to the tables, which were erected on a rising ground in the rear of the platform, and partook of the abundant supply which covered them." The food was distributed by the ladies in white, members of the "Legion of Honor," and by the Marshals.

Afternoon speakers included John Pierpont of Boston, Frederick Douglass of Lynn, James Freeman Clarke of Boston, William A. White of Watertown, the Reverends Howe and Russell of Hingham, Henry Clapp, Jr., of Lynn, the venerable Seth Sprague of Duxbury, and Oliver Johnson of New York.

*The Liberator* reported: "Music played an important part of the day." The paper described "the renowned Hutchinson Family singers" singing several songs, as well as the singing of the Hingham Anti-Slavery Choir, and said that all in the "immense audience" of an estimated 6,000–8,000 (reports of the numbers varied) listened intently.

The great Pic Nic concluded, according to *The Liberator*, when delegates and those assembled departed about 7 p.m., "satisfied that a good work had been accomplished for the cause; and gratified with the amount of enjoyment which had been experienced." The newspaper remarked that it was an unforgettable occasion for those attending, as well as for the Town, and gave much credit to the Hingham Ladies "for the ability and taste displayed in the arrangement and embellishment of the tables and decoration of the Grove," as well as to everyone attending for the interest shown in the Celebration.

*The Liberator*'s accounts of the day concluded in the description of the Town-wide decoration and participation. Bells throughout the town were rung at sunrise, noon, and sunset, and flags were displayed across the principal streets and along the route of the procession. Storefronts along the route were also "handsomely decorated with goods of brilliant colors."

Tranquility Grove itself was decorated by the activity of the friends in Hingham "with many mottoes appropriate to the occasion, fastened between its beautiful oaks, forming noble triumphal arches for the entering Procession." Among them were these:

"Shall a Republic which could not bear the bonds of a king cradle a bondage which a king has abolished?" An abolitionist banner carried in the August 1 processions. (*Collection of Massachusetts Historical Society*)

Rev. Mr. Oliver Stearns of Third Congregational Church, Hingham. (*Collection of Hingham Historical Society*)

For information about other electronic banking fees please see section 10 titled "Electronic Banking Fees" of the Card Agreement.

## Dollar Limits on Transactions

When you use your Card at ATMs and for purchase transactions, we may apply two daily limits to the amount you are authorized to withdraw from your deposit accounts during each day - a cash limit and a purchase limit.

We may issue authorizations, and permit withdrawals and purchases, in excess of these limits. The limits are based on your relationship with us and the type of Card you have with us.

We may establish higher or lower limits. Unless we have established another limit for you, your limit is set forth below. Please review section 6 titled "Dollar Limits on Transactions" of the Card Agreement carefully.

Cash Limit. The cash limit is the total amount you are authorized to withdraw each day from your deposit accounts at ATMs using your Card. Please note that some ATMs may not be able to dispense the full amount of your cash limit in a single transaction in which case you may need to perform more than one transaction.

| Type of Card | Daily Cash Limit is the lesser of your available balance or: |
| --- | --- |
| ATM Card | $700 |
| Business ATM Card | $700 |
| Debit Card/Access Device | $1,000 |

Purchase Limit. The purchase limit is the total amount of goods or services you are authorized to pay for each day from your deposit accounts by using your Card. Cash back you may receive from purchase transactions counts against your purchase limit. Cash back also includes: (a) purchases of money orders, cashier's checks, or other similar instruments and other things of value and (b) cash you obtain from a financial institution. Your purchase limit is generally in addition to your cash limit. For security purposes, we may place other restrictions on the purchase limit from time to time. The daily purchase limit on your ATM Card and Business ATM Card is $1,000. The daily purchase limit on your debit card or Access Card and Business ATM Card is $1,000. The daily purchase limit on your debit card or Access Device is your available balance.

In addition, when you use a Non-Bank of America ATM, you may be charged a fee by the ATM operator or any network used and you may be charged a fee for a balance inquiry even if you do not complete a fund transfer.

DTK-046691

# Schedule of Electronic Fees and Dollar Limits on Transactions Supplement to Your Card Agreement

Personal Debit Cards, Personal ATM Cards, Business ATM Cards, and Access Devices

Effective May 19, 2017 for Cards associated with deposit accounts opened at Bank of America in Arkansas, California, Colorado, Connecticut, Delaware, District of Columbia, Georgia, Idaho, Illinois, Indiana, Iowa, Kansas, Maine, Maryland, Massachusetts, Michigan, Minnesota, Missouri, Nevada, New Hampshire, New Jersey, New Mexico, New York, North Carolina, Oklahoma, Oregon, Pennsylvania, Rhode Island, South Carolina, Tennessee, Texas, Virginia and Washington.

This Schedule of Electronic Fees and Dollar Limits on Transactions Supplement to Your Card Agreement ("Schedule") supplements your Important Information Brochure: Card Agreement and Disclosure (the "Card Agreement") and is part of your contract with us for use of your Card. It applies to use of a Bank of America personal debit card, ATM Card, Business ATM or Access Device ("Card") that is linked to a deposit account opened in Arkansas, California, Colorado, Connecticut, Delaware, District of Columbia, Georgia, Idaho, Illinois, Indiana, Iowa, Kansas, Maine, Maryland, Massachusetts, Michigan, Minnesota, Missouri, Nevada, New Hampshire, New Jersey, New Mexico, New York, North Carolina, Oklahoma, Oregon, Pennsylvania, Rhode Island, South Carolina, Tennessee, Texas, Virginia and Washington. This Schedule contains information about the fees that apply to transactions at ATMs and the dollar limits that apply to the amount that you are authorized to withdraw from your deposit accounts each day. For other terms and conditions governing the use of your Card, please see the Card Agreement (Important Information Brochure: Card Agreement and Disclosure). We may change this Schedule at any time.

## Fees

The fees listed below apply to ATM and other transactions.

Bank of America ATM. A Bank of America ATM is an ATM that prominently displays the Bank of America name and logo on the ATM. When you use your Card at a Bank of America ATM, there are no ATM fees for withdrawals, deposits, transfers, and payments (Account fees, such as overdraft and excess transaction fees may apply).

Non-Bank of America ATM. A Non-Bank of America ATM is an ATM that does not prominently display the Bank of America name and logo on the ATM. When you use your Card for transactions at Non-Bank of America ATMs, we charge:

| | |
|---|---|
| Withdrawal, transfer and balance inquiry at a Non-Bank of America ATM located in the United States and U.S. territories, each. | $2.50* |
| Withdrawal, transfer and balance inquiry at a Non-Bank of America ATM located in a foreign country, each | $5.00* |
| Non-Bank of America Teller Withdrawal Fee - For each transaction, Fee applies when you authorize another financial institution to use your card number the greater of $5.00 OR 3% of the dollar amount to conduct a transaction (such as a withdrawal, transfer, or payment); and the other financial institution processes the transaction as a cash disbursement | of the transaction, up to a maximum of $10.00* |

(* These fees do not apply if you are a personal account holder and a U.S. Trust, Bank of America Private Wealth Management Client or Merrill Lynch Wealth Management Client who maintains a certain asset level.)

Hail! friend of Truth, thou enterest here
The grove long named TRANQUILLITY,
O let thy soul then breathe sweet peace
Pure love and TRUE HUMILITY.

True freedom is to share
All the chains our brothers wear.
West India Emancipation.
1st August, 1834.

True Freedom is to be
Earnest to make others free.

God made us free; then fetter not a brother's
limbs—

Many others were "equally appropriate and beautiful."

*The Liberator* also printed letters from Charles Francis Adams and from John Quincy Adams, which had been sent to Anna Quincy Thaxter for the celebration. These were read to the throng following Reverend Oliver Stearns's opening prayers.

"Hail! friend of Truth, thou enterest here The grove long named Tranquillity, O Let thy soul then breath sweet peace, Pure love and True Humility." This original 1844 banner welcomed delegates at the entrance to Tranquility Grove. (*Collection of Hingham Historical Society*)

"True Freedom is to be Earnest to make others free." Another banner that hung in the oak trees in Tranquility Grove in 1844. (*Collection of Hingham Historical Society*)

"God made us free! Then fetter not a brother's limbs." An original banner that hung in the oak trees of Tranquility Grove for the August 1 celebrations in 1844.
(*Collection of Hingham Historical Society*)

## From the *Hingham Patriot*

The *Hingham Patriot* account of the celebration appeared in the August 16 edition, in an article submitted anonymously. For some unexplained reason, the *Hingham Patriot* did not have a reporter or writer prepared to submit an article the previous week. Unlike *The Liberator*'s report, which was a factual account, the *Hingham Patriot* provided an editorial submitted by the anonymous "A Looker On," full of exclamation and enthusiasm and even approaching rapture. The *Hingham Patriot* did insert a veiled criticism for those who attended primarily to fill themselves with the food provided. A portion of the editorial is included here:

West India Emancipation

The Union Celebration of West India Emancipation by Plymouth, Norfolk, Suffolk and Essex Counties, which took place on the 2nd of August, was a grand and imposing occasion. To those who could revert to the day of small things in Anti-Slavery annals, when ten or twelve women assembled, in 1835, in the Vestry of the Baptist Church, in the midst of obloquy and persecution, and bound themselves, by a solemn pledge, to use all Christian and pacific means for the abolition of American slavery, this was a day of heart-thrilling and unutterable interest and satisfaction. To witness our fellow citizens coming up from the neighboring and more remote towns by hundreds and thousands, with music and banners, and the mingled voice of Thanksgiving and lamentation, to sympathise with, and encourage our high endeavor, and holy joy, this was a satisfaction too pure and deep to find, or even seek for utterance. We feel that it is the "Lord's doing and it is marvelous in our eyes."

The *Hingham Patriot* left the description of the details of the celebration, the procession, "the chaste and beautiful decorations of the tables, and the grove," "to those who had leisure of heart and head to observe them." Some of the mottos were described as "peculiarly appropriate and expressive—especially the one at the entrance through which the procession passed."

Welcome ALL to Freedom's altar,
Prayer-strengthen'd for the trial, come together,
Gird on the armor for the moral fight,
And, with the blessing of your Heavenly Father
MAINTAIN THE RIGHT.

Another:

Act, act in the living present,
Heart within, and God o'er head.

The *Hingham Patriot* account listed all the speakers, and added names to those chronicled by *The Liberator*. The journal added a description of the musical events.

"Welcome All to Freedom's Altar." Another of the original Tranquility Grove banners. (*Collection of Hingham Historical Society*)

The newspaper mentioned that William Lloyd Garrison was appointed President of the day, after which the exercises were opened with prayer by Mr. Stearns. A letter, from Hon. John Quincy Adams, was then read by the President, and "listened to with intense interest by the immense multitude." The first speaker was Edmund Quincy, who next addressed the meeting. He was followed successively by Messrs. Pierpont, Frederick Douglas, and Jas. Freeman Clark of Boston; Henry Clapp of Lynn, John L. Russell of South Hingham, Sereno Howe, and Lemuel Daggett of Hingham; and Hon. Seth Sprague of Duxbury, Wm. A. White of Watertown, and Oliver Johnson of New York.

The *Patriot* then described the music of the day: "... the exquisitely simple, sweet and soul-thrilling strains of the Hutchinsons were heard at intervals during these speeches, making the heart glad, the purpose strong, and the spirit devoted." In addition, Almira Seymour had written "an appropriate and beautiful song for the occasion," which was sung by Nathan Lincoln.

The lyric newspaper editorial added more to the day's description: "... a cloud now and then flitted across the bright azure of our joy; but it soon dispersed, and permanent sunshine was the character of the day. It is computed that not less than six thousand persons were present...". *The Hingham Patriot* jabbed in its anonymous editorial submitted by "A Looker On" at those who were there for an abundance of food rather than an abundance of spiritual nourishment:

Can those who gathered themselves together with the earnest desire to strengthen each other's hands and encourage each other's hearts, in the great moral conflict of truth and right, grudge them the pitiful gratification of lingering round the flesh-pots of Egypt, even until they were entirely emptied? We rather rejoice that these flesh-pots were so bountifully supplied by the good people of Hingham, and other towns; and that while the taste for the true and the pure was finding full and satisfying nutriment, those who thinking only what and how much they could eat, were not sent empty away. A LOOKER ON

## Hingham's Great Day Remembered

Called the largest abolitionist picnic ever held, the events of August 2, 1844 were also remembered as one of Hingham's great occasions of the 1800s. In 1912, almost sixty-five years later, Hingham resident Andrew J. Clark wrote a letter to the *Hingham Journal* entitled "Hingham's Great Day," recalling his excitement in participating in the event as a boy. This later account brings even more detailed description of the day's events. Clark remembered two steamboats landing "at the extreme end of the driveway on the estate of the late Alfred Hersey, directly opposite the Blake residence on Summer Street," the procession, the "several bands of music," and the banners.

The way to Tranquility Grove, he said, was "through South and Main streets ... into a private passageway on the Willard estate that led at that time up and across what is now Central street ... to Tranquility Grove."

The Thaxter brothers' property belonged in part to Susan Barker Willard, a granddaughter of Henry Thaxter and great-niece of Edward Thaxter in the early 1900s. She would eventually sell the property to endow the Hingham Historical Society.

"Here," Clark said, "they held a monster picnic. Long tables were loaded with edibles, such as were usually found at an old fashioned picnic. These tables were roped off from the big gathering. But many waiters passed up and down inside the ropes with plates and platers [*sic.*] filled with good things to eat, others passed mugs of coffee and lemonade. All was eagerly seized and devoured by the people outside the ropes."

"Hingham has always been known for its generosity in entertaining people as their guests on all such occasions, so it is needless to add that there was an abundance for all who were present at the grove." Clark concluded that there was "singing and speaking galore" after the collation, but he had been too young to understand it. Nonetheless, said he, "I shall always remember Hingham's Great Day."

Some years following Tranquility Grove events, the steamboat Governor Andrew, named for Massachusetts Civil War Governor Joseph Andrew of Hingham, departed regularly from the same steamboat pier used by the Portland in 1844. (*Collection of Hingham Historical Society*)

*Above:* Remnant of Steamboat Wharf in Hingham Harbor today.

*Below:* The 1844 procession walked to the left from North Street onto South Street at this intersection, and then turned left onto Main Street.

# 3

# Letters and Songs

Former President John Quincy Adams lived in Quincy at Peacefield, or "the Old House," the family estate that had been purchased by his parents, John and Abigail Adams. A member of Congress until his death in 1848, he spent his time at Peacefield in correspondence, gardening, the cultivation of trees, and writing in his journal each day. His fierce opposition to slavery led to his resistance to the Congressional gag rule that barred any discussion of slavery, and also to the Mexican-American War, the annexation of Texas, and the pro-slavery interests' effort to declare war on Great Britain for its opposition to slavery worldwide.

Adams's diary records his decision not to participate in the August 1 celebrations in Hingham, partially because of "age and infirmity." He had been approached by his Hingham cousin, Anna Quincy Thaxter, as well as by a Mr. Loring, both of Hingham, who urged him to participate. Adams wrote a letter "of some prolixity" to Thaxter, and Loring was deputized to deliver it.

## Diary of John Quincy Adams

On July 30, just three days before the Tranquility Grove Pic Nic, Adams noted in his journal:

> I wrote an answer to Miss Thaxter's invitation to me to attend the anniversary celebration of the 1st of August at Hingham.... We had a visit this afternoon ... from Mr. Loring who was very urgent in soliciting my attendance at the Hingham celebration of the 1st of August. I persisted in declining, assigned my lameness from which I have not sufficiently recovered, but thinking of some others, not less monitory to detain me at home. I told him I had answered with some prolixity Miss Thaxter's letter of invitation, and explained my unwillingness to take part in this anniversary. He said he should go to Boston again tomorrow, and on his return in the evening would stop and take the letter to Miss Thaxter and deliver it to her...

Quincy Tuesday 30 July 1844.

30. IV: 30. Tuesday.
Hülsemann Chevalier
Loving Thomas.

The preconcerted current of my daily occupations continues under great perturbation. My Son went to Boston this day and brought me out a volume of critical and miscellaneous Essays of T. Babington Macaulay, consisting of reprinted articles from the Edinburgh Review. I wanted it for an article upon Lord Bacon, of which I had heard, and which I expect will be satisfactory. It is a review of a new Edition of Bacon's works in 16 octavo volumes, published 1825–1834, by Basil Montagu—and in the last volume of which there is the desideratum, a new Life of Bacon. I sent an answer to Mr Daniel S. Parker's invitation to me to visit the Ship which he has called by my name, and promised to go next Saturday, if a fair day. And I wrote an answer to Miss Thaxter's invitation to me to attend the anniversary celebration of the 1st of August, at Hingham. We had a visit this afternoon from Mr Hülsemann the Austrian Chargé d'Affaires at Washington; and afterwards one from Mr Loving who was very urgent in soliciting my attendance at the Hingham celebration of the 1st of August. I persisted in declining, assigned my lameness from which I have not yet sufficiently recovered, as my principal reason, but hinting at some others, not less monitory to detain me at home—I told him I had answered with some prolixity Miss Thaxter's Letter of invitation, and explained my unwillingness to take part in the celebration of this anniversary. He said he should go to Boston again to-morrow, and on his return in the evening would stop and take the Letter to Miss Thaxter and deliver it to her—I began to read the Sylva Sylvarum, or Natural History in ten Centuries: each consisting of 100 experiments—There is a preface to this work by William Brawley Lord Bacon's Secretary written for publication before his death, but not published till after that event—He says it was intended as a third part of the Instauration. As a middle link between the De Augmentis Scientiarum, and the Novum Organum. But Bacon hesitated whether to publish it or not during his life time, and it does not appear at all essential to the great work. It is divided into experiments in consort, and experiments solitary; and it has more the appearance of a cookery book, or collection of Confectioner's receipts than a philosophical system of Natural History—It begins with experiments of percolation—or the straining and passing of bodies one through another—And the remarkable fact is that he falsifies the result of the experiment. He says dig a pit on the Sea shore above high water mark and sink it below low water mark—As the tide flows in it will fill with fresh and potable water. This is a mistake—The water will not be potable, nor even potable though it will lose many of its saline particles, by evaporation. Charles spent the evening here, but his wife did not come.

John Quincy Adams's journal for July 30, 1844, where he writes his regrets that he cannot attend the August 1 celebrations in Hingham. (*Collection of Massachusetts Historical Society*)

On the day of the West India Celebration in Hingham, Adams's long, complex, and urgent letter was read in its entirety to the throng. He rejoiced in the reason for the celebration and warned about those who were threatening Britain because of its effort to do away with slavery around the world, the annexation of Mexican territory, and suspect actions of President Tyler and Secretary of State John C. Calhoun.

The *Hingham Patriot* printed the entire letter from former President Adams. In spite of its "prolixity," it is reprinted in its entirety in this book in the Appendix, since it brings together so many of the seething concerns of the day. Adams talks about the reason for the celebration of August 1, lauds the action of the British Parliament, praises those celebrating the anniversary of the emancipation of slaves, warns of the potential perfidy of the United States government in attempting to overturn the actions of the British Parliament possibly leading to war, and his embarrassment at this, and expostulates about "slavemongering diplomacy" underway in Washington related to Texas, former Mexican territory, and California. Adams, although infirm, continued to represent the district in Congress until his death in Congress in 1848.

## Letter from John Quincy Adams

This is an excerpt of the letter written by John Quincy Adams, and read at the Celebration of the West India Emancipation, on August 2, in Hingham. The entire letter may be found in the Appendix.

Quincy, 29th July, 1844.

Miss Thaxter:

In declining the invitation which I received last summer to attend the celebration of the first of August, it was in no wise my intention to express disapprobation of the celebration itself. The abolition of slavery in the colonies of Great Britain, by the Parliament of that realm, was an event, at which, if the whole human race could have been concentrated in one person, the heart of that person would have leaped for joy. The restoration of 800,000 human beings from a state of degrading oppression to the rights bestowed upon them by the God of nature at their birth, was of itself a cause of rejoicing to the pure in heart throughout the habitable earth. But that is not the only nor the most radiant glory of that day. It was the pledge of Power and of Will of the mightiest nation upon the globe, that the bondage of man shall cease; that the manacle and the fetter shall drop from every limb; that the ties of nature shall no longer be outraged by man's inhumanity to man; that the self-evident truths of our Declaration of Independence shall not longer be idle mockeries, belied by the transcendent power of Slavery, welded into our Constitution. It was the voice of the herald, like that of John the Baptist in the wilderness, proclaiming, as with the trump of the archangel, that the standing fundamental policy of the British Empire was thenceforth the peaceable abolition of slavery throughout the world.

Well, then, may the friends of Freedom and of Man rejoice at the annual return of that day. Well may they, from far and wide, assemble and meet together in mutual gratulation at the return of so blessed a day. Well may they come in crowds to cheer and encourage one another to contribute, every one according to his ability, to the final consummation of this glorious and stupendous undertaking.... I cannot be with you, for age and infirmity forbid; but for every supplication breathed by you for the universal emancipation of man, and the extinction of slavery upon earth, my voice shall respond Amen!

From your faithful friend and kinsman,

John Quincy Adams

Charles Francis Adams of Quincy, John Quincy Adams's son and in 1844 a member of the Massachusetts legislature, sent a brief letter regretting his absence from the August 1 celebrations. It was also sent to his cousin, Anna Quincy Thaxter, "on behalf of the Committee of Arrangements for the celebration of the first of August at Hingham," read to the crowd following his father's letter, and later printed in the *Hingham Patriot* and *The Liberator*.

## Letter from Charles Francis Adams

Miss Anna Q. Thaxter, on behalf of the Committee of Arrangements for the celebration of the first of August at Hingham.

Quincy, July 29, 1844.

A brief excursion, from which I have but just returned, must be my apology for not answering sooner the invitation which has been very kindly extended to me, through you, to attend the celebration at Hingham, of the anniversary of the first of August.

My engagements are such that it will be out of my power to be present on that day. But, wherever I may be, and however occupied upon its annual recurrence during my life, I trust I shall never be unmindful of the great event which it commemorates, the most brilliant victory of a purely moral principle in political affairs that can be found recorded in the history of modern times.

With great respect, I remain,

Your obedient servant,

Charles Francis Adams

Frederick Douglass spoke at the Hingham events of August 2, 1844, as well as in Concord on August 1, following Ralph Waldo Emerson. His words were not recorded at either event. However, some twenty-three years later, Douglass spoke at another West India Celebration day in Canandaigua, New York. An excerpt of his speech that day samples his oratory, and suggests what he may have said in Hingham.

## Journal of Frederick Douglass

... such was the condition of our brothers and sisters in the British West Indies, up to the morning of the first of August, 1834. The wicked love of dominion by man over man, had made strong their fetters and multiplied their chains. But on the memorable morning which we are met to celebrate, one bolt from the moral sky of Britain left these bloodstained irons all scattered and broken throughout the West Indies, and the limbs they had bruised, out-stretched in praise and thanksgiving to God for deliverance. No man of any sensibility can read the account of that great transaction without emotions too great for utterance. There was something Godlike in this decree of the British nation. It was the spirit of the Son of God commanding the devil of slavery to go out of the British West Indies.

## "Hymn for the 1st of August," Almira Seymour

Acclaimed poet Almira Seymour of Hingham wrote the lyrics for a song for the August 1 celebration, appealing to Heaven to free the bound and chained captives. Sung by Nathan Lincoln of Hingham on August 2, it was printed in the *Hingham Patriot* of August 16, 1844, along with the general reports of the occasion. The words are both poetic and powerful, and include reference to the freed slaves of the West Indies, criticism of the United States where slavery still ruled, the cry of the oppressed slaves and terror of the tyrant, and a plea to God to convince the souls of slave-owners to repent. An excerpt is printed here, and the entire song appears in the Appendix.

> A voice o'er the wide blue sea—
>    A voice through New-England groves—
> A song for the ransomed Free,
>    Where a crowned head's subjects rove!
>
> A wail from fair Southern plains
>    The home of soft airs and flowers—
> A wail for the bound with chains,
>    In this boasted land of ours!
>
> A shout that the world shall hear—
>    A shout that shall reach to Heaven—
> Dried up is the captive's tear,
> And the captive's bonds are riven...

## Songs of the Hutchinson Family Singers

In the months leading up to the August 1 celebration, the widely popular Hutchinson Family Singers began to include anti-slavery songs in their concerts. Prior to this, they had sung temperance songs. Perhaps their best-known abolitionist ballad, "Get Off the Track," was published shortly before August, urging everyone to jump on Freedom's train. It surely was sung in Hingham that day. Jesse Hutchinson penned the words to the tune "Old Dan Tucker."

With many verses, the song chronicles the journey of the abolitionists leading to the day of emancipation, enthusiastically describing banners waving, the momentum of the effort, rolling through reluctant groups of professionals "Merchants, editors, physicians, Lawyers, priests and politicians." Politicians are dealt with along the way. The song warns them all to get on the train to emancipation or get run over. Based on a lively tune, it must have had the crowds clapping and singing along with huge enthusiasm. (The entire song appears in the Appendix.)

"Get Off the Track"

Ho! the car, Emancipation,
Rides majestic thro' our nation
Bearing on its train, the story Liberty! a nation's glory.
Roll it along! Roll it along!
Roll it along! thro' the nation
Freedom's car, Emancipation
Roll it along! Roll it along!
Roll it along! thro' the nation
Freedom's car, Emancipation.

First of all the train, and greater,
Speeds the dauntless Liberator
Onward cheered amid hosannas,
And the waving of free banners.
Roll it along! Roll it along!
Roll it along! spread your banners
While the people shout hosannas.
Men of various predilections,
Frightened, run in all directions;
Merchants, editors, physicians,
Lawyers, priests and politicians.
Get out of the way! Get out of the way!
Get out of the way! every station,
Clear the track of 'mancipation...

## Anti-Slavery Songbook of Jairus Lincoln

Members of the Hingham Anti-Slavery Choir participated with the crowd in Tranquility Grove singing songs from the *Anti-Slavery Melodies: For the Friends of Freedom*, gathered by Jairus Lincoln of Hingham, the Grand Marshal of the day, and published in 1843. Many of the songs were new words set to old melodies, written by well-known poets and abolitionists, including John Greenleaf Whittier.

Two anti-slavery songbooks preceded his, one collected by Maria Weston Chapman of Weymouth and Boston, who was a key Garrisonian activist, responsible for organizing many anti-slavery fairs to raise funds for the cause, and for finding special goods for the fairs from abolitionist supporters in Europe.

One well-known anti-slavery song, the "Song of the Abolitionist," is included in its entirety here. The words were written by William Lloyd Garrison to the familiar tune "Auld Lang Syne." Sung with pride by abolitionists, it became a battle cry, challenging all who might seek to discourage their sacred efforts.

1. I am an Abolitionist! I glory in the name;
   Though now by slavery's minions hissed, And covered o'er with shame;
   It is a spell of light and power, The watch-word of the free;
   Who spurns it in the trial-hour, A craven soul is he.
2. I am an Abolitionist! Then urge me not to pause,
   For joyfully do I enlist In Freedom's sacred cause;
   A nobler strife the world ne'er saw, Th'enslaved to disenthral;
   I am a soldier for the war, Whatever may befall.
3. I am an Abolitionist! Oppression's deadly foe;
   In God's great strength will I resist, And lay the monster low;
   In God's great name do I demand, To all be freedom given,
   That peace and joy may fill the land, And songs go up to heaven.
4. I am an Abolitionist! No threats shall awe my soul;
   No perils cause me to desist, No bribes my acts control;
   A freeman will I live and die, In sunshine and in shade, And raise my voice for liberty, Of nought on earth afraid.

*Above and opposite page:* Two pages of "I am an Abolitionist," written by William Lloyd Garrison, and part of the anti-slavery songbook.

71

# Song of the Abolitionist.

(CONTINUED.)

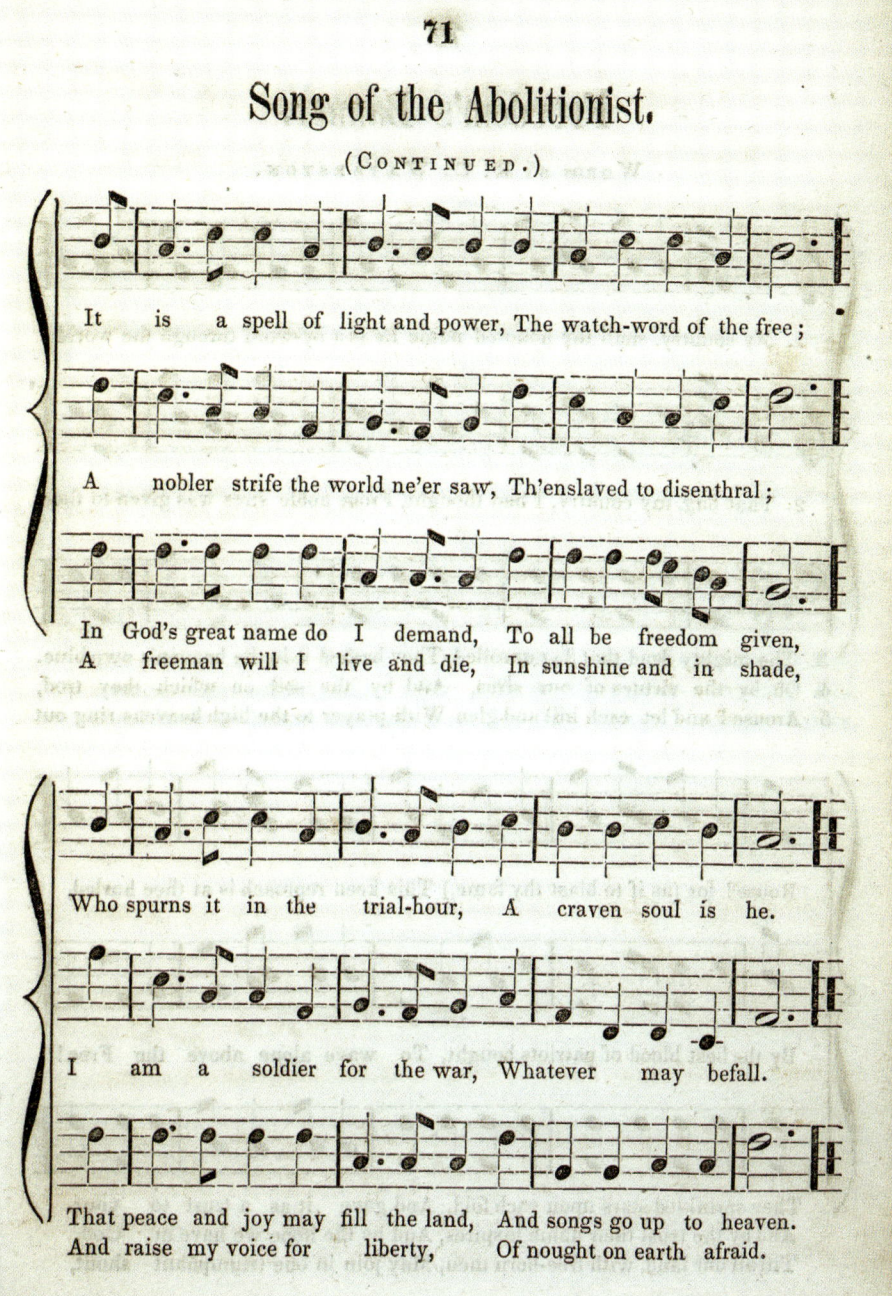

It    is    a spell of  light and power, The watch-word of  the free ;

A    nobler  strife the world ne'er saw, Th'enslaved to disenthral ;

In God's great name do  I   demand,  To all be  freedom  given,
A    freeman will I  live and die,  In sunshine and  in   shade,

Who spurns it   in   the     trial-hour,  A    craven soul  is  he.

I    am   a   soldier  for the war, Whatever     may  befall.

That peace and  joy may  fill  the land,  And songs go up  to  heaven.
And  raise my voice for     liberty,       Of nought on earth  afraid.

# ANTI-SLAVERY

# MELODIES:

FOR

# THE FRIENDS OF FREEDOM.

PREPARED FOR

# THE HINGHAM ANTI-SLAVERY SOCIETY,

BY JAIRUS LINCOLN.

HINGHAM:

PUBLISHED BY ELIJAH B. GILL.

Price 25 cents.

Title page of *Anti-Slavery Melodies*, prepared by Jairus Lincoln in 1843. (*Collection of Massachusetts Historical Society*)

# 4

# Anti-Slavery Pic Nic Participants

News accounts in the *Hingham Patriot* and in the abolitionist newspaper *The Liberator* had identified individuals who led the ceremonies, and participated in the speeches and music and letters of the day at Tranquility Grove. John Wallace Hutchinson, of the Hutchinson Family Singers, mentioned additional speakers in his autobiography, who had not been noted in the news articles.

Speakers, both black and white, came from the heart of the radical abolitionist movement, the Boston "clique" that gathered around William Lloyd Garrison, and were influential across the nation. They organized anti-slavery fairs and events, such as the West Indian Emancipation Pic Nic on August 2, 1844, to raise funds and spread the word against slavery. They organized anti-slavery societies, ran newspapers in Boston and New York, sent petitions to Congress and to the State House, and participated in other anti-slavery journals. Their journal offices provided important sources of support and organization for the Underground Railroad.

From time to time, the focus of the abolitionists would change, and Garrison's colleagues would occasionally split off to form another, sometimes rival organization. The year 1844 was a presidential election year as well, which added fuel to the abolitionist fires with speeches delivered in Hingham that day.

These biographical sketches include photographs of the speakers, which, for the most part, were taken years after the 1844 Pic Nic, when they significantly older. The exception is Frederick Douglass, whose 160 photographs and daguerreotypes date back as early as 1841.

## Marshal: Jairus Lincoln

Hingham's Jairus Lincoln, whose long life ran from 1792 to 1890, was a schoolmaster, an abolitionist and a key organizer of the August 2 Pic Nic at Tranquility Grove. Early announcements in the *Hingham Patriot* include his name.

He was also a composer and compiler of *Anti-Slavery Melodies: For the Friends of Freedom*, prepared in 1843 for the Hingham Anti-Slavery Choir, in anticipation of the

John Greenleaf Whittier, a Quaker and abolitionist, and long-time friend of Garrison, wrote poems set to music for *Anti-Slavery Melodies*. (*Collection of Library of Congress*)

big picnic and rally in 1844. The songbook included songs with words by William Lloyd Garrison, John Greenleaf Whittier, and other abolitionists and well-known poets, often harshly drawn against a nation that could tolerate slavery. To "Auld Lang Syne," for instance, Garrison wrote the song, "I am an Abolitionist!" described above.

*Anti-Slavery Melodies* was published by Elijah Gill of the *Hingham Patriot* in February 1843. Lincoln hoped to inspire every town to create an anti-slavery choir. The songbook was prepared both for the Hingham Anti-Slavery Society and for the "Friends of Freedom." Some of the songs came from collections published the year before in "The Liberty and Anti-Slavery Song Book," and the "Anti-Slavery Picknick."

The "History Engine" linked with a University of Richmond course on "Transatlantic Abolitionism" describes the importance of the strong language used in abolitionist hymns and songs, reflecting their militant position:

> Along with the martial imagery in the "Song of the Abolitionist" are images of persuasion and argument. The many references to God, "In God's great name do I demand" and the use of words like soul or peace and joy, depicts many abolitionists' hope that by appealing to slaveholders on moral grounds that slavery would come to an end. The lyrics of the song emphasized the tactic of moral advocacy, but beside this moral plea was the hint of the militant words that foreshadowed the rise of more violent means of abolitionism that would soon come to the forefront only a decade later with the actions of people like John Brown at Harper's Ferry.

A savage parody of "My Country! 'tis of thee" included these words:

> My native country! Thee,
> Where all men are born free,
> If white their skin:
> I love thy hills and dales,
> Thy mounts and pleasant vales
> But hate thy negro sales
> As foulest sin…

Jairus Lincoln had arrived in Hingham in about 1830 with his wife, Mary Cotton Ware, who was the daughter of Henry Ware, formerly the minister at Hingham's ancient Old Ship Church. Lincoln was a member of the Hingham School Committee and Secretary of the Hingham Cemetery Corporation for several years until 1844. Born in Boston in 1794, Lincoln left Hingham in 1846, moved to Northborough where he continued his anti-slavery efforts, including lobbying against the annexation of Texas, and farmed the land until his death in 1882.

## President of the Day: William Lloyd Garrison

William Lloyd Garrison, 1805–1879, was the founder and central figure of the Boston abolitionists and a leader of the national movement. He founded *The Liberator*, the Boston anti-slavery newspaper, in 1830, and helped form the New England Anti-Slavery

William Lloyd Garrison. (*Collection of Massachusetts Historical Society*)

Society in 1832. Garrison was a radical abolitionist who saw the Constitution as a pro-slavery document, advocated disunion as a result, and pushed for the immediate abolition of slavery.

In his first issue of *The Liberator*, Garrison said, "I do not wish to think, or speak, or write, with moderation.... I am in earnest—I will not equivocate—I will not excuse—I will not retreat a single inch—AND I WILL BE HEARD." This rallying cry was printed on one of the banners paraded through Hingham in 1844.

Garrison was heard. For more than three decades, from the first issue of his weekly paper in 1831, until after the end of the Civil War in 1865 when the last issue was published, Garrison spoke out eloquently and passionately against slavery and for the rights of America's black inhabitants.

## Vice-Presidents: Bourne Spooner, Robert Purvis

Bourne Spooner, 1790–1870, who lived in Plymouth, was the founder of the Plymouth Cordage Company. An active abolitionist, along with his wife Hannah, he provided hospitality in his home to Garrison, Phillips, Douglass, and others. He was a close friend of Garrison and President of the Old Colony Anti-Slavery Society. Spooner was most likely involved with the Underground Railroad activity when fugitive slaves landed in Plymouth.

Robert Purvis, 1810–1898, of Philadelphia, was the son of a white merchant in South Carolina, and a free black woman. He was educated at the Pennsylvania Abolition

Bourne Spooner.
(*Collection of Massachusetts Historical Society*)

Robert Purvis.
(*Collection of Massachusetts Historical Society*)

Society's Clarkson School and at Amherst College. Purvis was the unofficial "President of the Underground Railroad," which helped and housed an estimated 11,000 fugitive slaves, "newly freed souls," over the course of thirty years. He was a founding member of Garrison's American Anti-Slavery Society and was active in abolitionist efforts in the U.S. and Great Britain.

## Opening Prayer: Rev. Mr. Oliver Stearns

Rev. Mr. Oliver Stearns, 1807–1872, was the third Minister of the Third Congregational Society (Hingham's New North Church) from 1839 to 1856. An abolitionist, he was described as scholarly and learned and of great character. When the Plymouth Anti-Slavery Society voted to end racial segregation at his urging in 1841, Lucretia Leonard, the only African-American in his congregation, came down from the "slave gallery," and joined her employers, the Thaxter sisters, also abolitionists, in their pew. The church, located in Fountain Square, was the gathering place for the 1844 procession through the Town of Hingham to the Steamboat Landing and then to Tranquility Grove. His well-known 1851 sermon against the Fugitive Slave Act, "The Gospel applied to the Fugitive Slave Law," was published and distributed throughout the nation at the initiative of his parishioners.

## Letters: John Quincy Adams, Charles Francis Adams

John Quincy Adams, 1767–1848, of Quincy, a son of John and Abigail Adams, had been Secretary of State during the Monroe Administration, the sixth President of the United States, a diplomat, and a member of the U.S. Senate. In 1844, he was Hingham's congressman in the House of Representatives. He was also the most prominent national figure opposing slavery at the time of the Hingham Pic Nic of 1844. Although, as mentioned earlier, he had been invited to participate in the event a year before by his cousin, Anna Quincy Thaxter, he declined because of his health, and instead sent the long letter, which was read as the first order of the day.

In Congress, Adams opposed annexation of Texas, railed against the gag rule (where all petitions involving slavery were laid on the table without discussion, and no further action was to be taken), and engaged in heated debates with pro-slavery colleagues. The American Anti-Slavery Society had begun submitting petitions calling for the abolition of slavery in the 1830s. The "gag rule" was passed by Congress in 1836. Adams called for the abolition of the gag rule, saying that it was unconstitutional. One of his petitions was submitted by twenty-two slaves, creating great consternation in Congress. The gag rule was overturned in 1844, thanks to his persistence.

Adams described sitting for the painting of one of his portraits, included below, in his journal entry of September 17, 1844, just six weeks after the events in Hingham. This portrait hangs in the National Portrait Gallery in Washington, D.C., today. He was introduced to the portrait painter by his cousin, Thomas Loring of Hingham:

> Mr. Loring called here this morning with Mr. Hudson a portrait painter residing at
> Hingham and desirous of painting a picture of me—I gave him accordingly a sitting of

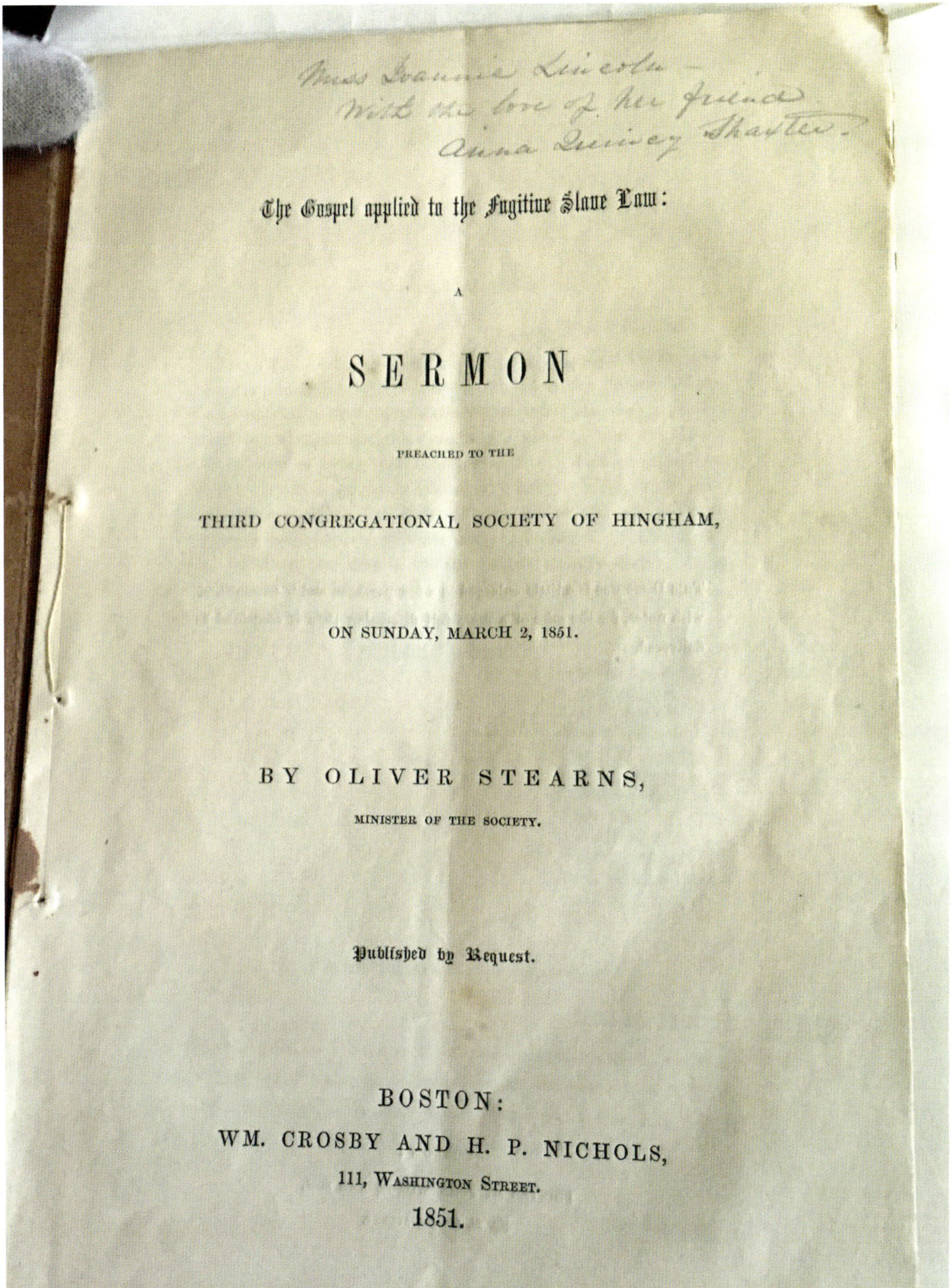

*Miss Joannie Lincoln —
With the love of her friend
Anna Quincy Thaxter.*

## The Gospel applied to the Fugitive Slave Law:

A

# SERMON

PREACHED TO THE

### THIRD CONGREGATIONAL SOCIETY OF HINGHAM,

ON SUNDAY, MARCH 2, 1851.

## BY OLIVER STEARNS,

MINISTER OF THE SOCIETY.

Published by Request.

## BOSTON:
### WM. CROSBY AND H. P. NICHOLS,
111, WASHINGTON STREET.
1851.

Title page of Sermon opposed to the Fugitive Slave Act, given by Rev. Stearns on March 2, 1851. A gift of Anna Quincy Thaxter to a friend. (*Collection of Hingham Historical Society*) an hour and a half, and he dined with us. I could not keep my eyes open half the time while I was sitting. Mr. Loring brought us a basket of Seek No Further apples, and proceeded to Boston...

On September 19, the painter, William Hudson, Jr., was back for another sitting of an hour, and this was followed the next Monday by a sitting from 10 a.m. to noon, during which time Adams reviewed his correspondence. On Tuesday, September 24, Hudson returned and was greeted with mild irritation:

Mr. Hudson came and took a sitting for my portrait. It is so irksome and so time-consuming that he has agreed to reduce the sittings to one hour a day, and I have agreed to give him as many sittings as he shall desire. He improved the likeness very much this day.

Hudson returned on Wednesday, September 25 for an hour's sitting. Adams wrote: "He inclines to take the hands, and we had a long conversation how to dispose of them." Adams was suffering from rheumatism, which affected his hands with some swelling and disfigurement. In his portrait, he holds a spyglass, which helps to mask his left hand. His right hand is portrayed across his chest and inside his coat. It is not visible. On Friday, September 27, Adams made mention of the arrangement, in a final note of approval:

Mr Hudson came for another sitting of my portrait which he has so much improved that the family are all pleased with the likeness. The spy-glass in the hand will distinguish it from all the other portraits of me.

On the day of the first portrait sitting, September 17, Adams was approached by a Special Committee from the Whig Convention of the 8th Congressional District to tell him that he had been unanimously nominated for the Office of Representative in the 29th Congress. He wrote: "... although my age and infirmities had led me to hesitate whether I should prove sufficient to discharge all the duties of the office, I must hope for improved health, and in the crisis impending over the country, accepted the nomination." November 1844 brought the election of James Polk, and Adams wrote: "It is the victory of the Slavery Element in the Constitution of the United States." Though he considered leaving public service at that low point, he would serve four more years, until his death on the floor of Congress in 1848.

Charles Francis Adams, 1807–1886, of Quincy, was a member of Congress, Ambassador to Great Britain during the Civil War, biographer of his grandfather John Adams, and his father, John Quincy Adams. He later became the candidate for Vice-President of the Free Soil Party (1848). He did not attend the Hingham event, but sent a brief letter, which was also published in the *Hingham Patriot* and *The Liberator*. At the time of the event, he was a member of the Massachusetts House of Representatives.

John Quincy Adams. Portrait by
William Hudson, Jr., of Hingham,
painted in September 1844 at
the request of Thomas Loring
of Hingham, Adams's cousin.
(*Collection of the National Portrait
Gallery*)

Charles Francis Adams. (*Collection
of Massachusetts Historical Society*)

## The Keynote Address, and Afternoon Speakers

Edmund Quincy, 1808–1877, of Dedham and Boston, who delivered the major address of the morning, was an editor active in the Massachusetts Anti-Slavery Society and abolitionist organizations. He was an editor of *The Liberator* and other abolitionist journals. His father, Josiah Quincy III, had been a congressman and Mayor of Boston, and was President of Harvard in 1844. Quincy was among the Garrison Boston "clique" who organized anti-slavery events, published anti-slavery newspapers in Boston and New York, and provided stations for the Underground Railroad. He was a close friend of Wendell Phillips.

John Pierpont, 1785–1866, was Minister at the Hollis Street Church in Boston, as well as an abolitionist, poet, and writer. His songs and poems were often recited at antislavery meetings and events, and his words were printed in Jairus Lincoln's book of anti-slavery songs, used at the Hingham event.

Frederick Douglass, 1818–1895, was living in Lynn at the time of the Hingham event. A fugitive slave, he had escaped in 1836 and made his way to New Bedford. He subscribed to *The Liberator*, and attended abolitionist meetings. In 1841, he spoke up at the Massachusetts Anti-Slavery Annual Conference in Nantucket, where, it was said: "Flinty hearts were pierced and cold ones melted by his eloquence." He was recruited by the abolitionists to become a lecturer against slavery, and told his full story and published his autobiography in 1845. Douglass lectured in Great Britain after the publication of his autobiography, seeking safety there from re-enslavement. His freedom was purchased by some of his supporters for $711.00 in 1846. In later years, he would be physically threatened and beaten on the lecture circuit. He eventually separated from the Garrison group because of differences in philosophy. Douglass's writings and lectures inspired many thousands over the years, and continue to do so today.

Rev. James Freeman Clarke, 1810–1888, of Boston was an ordained Unitarian minister, an abolitionist, an essayist, and a writer. He established the Church of the Disciples in 1841, applying "Christian religion to social problems of the day," and later became secretary of the Unitarian Association, and a professor at Harvard Divinity School. He was one of the Transcendentalists, and saw himself as a spiritual peacemaker. He was not considered one of the radical abolitionists.

William Abijah White, 1818–1856, born in Watertown, was a Harvard graduate and a lawyer. James Russell Lowell's brother-in-law, White was a close friend of Frederick Douglass, with whom he lectured in the Midwest in the 1850s. He saved Douglass's life at a raucous rally when participants beat the speakers. An anti-slavery spokesman and editor, he eventually moved to Wisconsin, where he died under mysterious circumstances.

Rev. Sereno Howe was the minister of the First Baptist Church of Hingham from 1842–1849. First Baptist Church welcomed Frederick Douglass as a speaker in 1842, and Angelina Grimke at about the same time.

Rev. John L. Russell was the minister of Hingham's Second Parish Church for two terms and was described as an "earnest and uncompromising opponent of American slavery, at a time when slavery had many and powerful apologists in the Northern states." Russell was born in Salem. A Harvard graduate, interested in theological studies and nature, Russell was said to be blunt and "extremely outspoken."

Edmund Quincy. (*Collection of Massachusetts Historical Society*)

John Pierpont. (*Collection of Massachusetts Historical Society*)

Frederick Douglass. (*Collection of the Onondaga Historical Association*)

James Freeman Clarke. (*Collection of Massachusetts Historical Society*)

Rev. Lemuel Daggett, was Minister to the Methodist Episcopal Church Meeting House in Hingham.

Henry Clapp, Jr., 1814–1875, of Lynn, was an "outspoken" abolitionist editor and an outright anarchist who did not believe in any institutions at all, let alone slavery.

Venerable Seth Sprague lived in Duxbury. There were two distinguished citizens of Duxbury with the name of Seth Sprague, father and son. The senior Seth Sprague had been a farmer and a fisherman, a member of the Massachusetts legislature, and active in the Revolution and the War of 1812 in matters of shipping and shipbuilding. He became an abolitionist and petitioned the Methodist Episcopal Church not to support slavery. He and other abolitionists separated from that church to form the Wesleyan Church. Sprague had fifteen children and passed away in his mid-eighties in 1847.

Oliver Johnson, 1809–1889, of New York, was called an "abolitionist and reformer." He was an editor and writer for major anti-slavery newspapers in the United States and a Quaker with a passion to end slavery. He was an aide to and follower of William Lloyd Garrison and also involved in numerous progressive movements on other issues of the day.

John Wallace Hutchinson's autobiography includes an augmented account of those who spoke during the afternoon of August 2 at Tranquility Grove in Hingham. These additional names follow his words:

> On another day twelve hundred of the finest spirits of the age went to Hingham for a great open-air convention, Garrison, Phillips, Douglass, Clapp, Charles C. Burleigh, Charles Lenox Remond, George Bradburn, Parker Pillsbury, Robert Purvis of Philadelphia, Stephen Foster, Abby Kelley, Francis Jackson, Edmund Quincy and others spoke.

Wendell Phillips, 1811–1884, a Boston Brahmin, graduated from Harvard and Harvard Law School, and was an extraordinarily compelling orator and abolitionist, who worked closely with Garrison. He wrote for the anti-slavery newspapers, built a national reputation, and lectured at abolitionist events across the country.

Charles Calistus Burleigh, 1810–1878, originally from Connecticut, became an abolitionist editor and wrote for *The Liberator*, as well as for the *Pennsylvania Freeman*, the abolitionist paper of the Eastern Pennsylvania Anti-Slavery Society. He grew a long beard, which he declared he would not remove until the liberation of the slaves in the United States.

Charles Lenox Remond, 1810–1873, was born to free black parents in Salem, Massachusetts, and became one of the earliest black abolitionist speakers. In 1840, he traveled with Garrison to speak at the World Anti-Slavery Society in London.

Rev. George Bradburn, 1806–1880, was born in Attleboro, Massachusetts, and educated at Exeter and the Harvard Divinity School. He was a politician and Unitarian minister, who lectured widely as an abolitionist. He traveled with a group of the Boston abolitionists to London to the World Anti-Slavery Convention, and joined Garrison and the others in meeting the anti-slavery group in Europe, including Daniel O'Connell of Ireland. He also joined Frederick Douglass and William A. White on a lecture tour of "100 conventions" beginning in 1843.

Rev. Parker Pillsbury, 1809–1898, was born in Hamilton, Massachusetts, and moved to New Hampshire, where he farmed until he was called to become a minister.

Oliver Johnson. (*Collection of Massachusetts Historical Society*)

Wendell Phillips. (*Collection of Massachusetts Historical Society*)

Charles Calistus Burleigh. (*Collection of Massachusetts Historical Society*)

Charles Lenox Remond. (*Collection of Massachusetts Historical Society*)

He became a strong abolitionist and alienated his congregation with his views. Over the years, he wrote for and edited various anti-slavery journals and was active in the anti-slavery societies.

Stephen Symonds Foster, 1809–1881, born in New Hampshire, became an abolitionist when he attended Dartmouth. He was outspoken in his criticism of churches, during their services, when they would not condemn slavery, and left his calling as a minister to become a traveling lecturer for anti-slavery societies. He married abolitionist Abby Kelly the year following the Tranquility Grove Pic Nic, and they moved to Worcester, where they provided refuge for fugitive slaves.

Abby Kelley, 1811–1887, was born in Pelham, Massachusetts. Brought up a Quaker, she received a Quaker education and taught in Lynn, where she was introduced to the anti-slavery movement. After hearing Garrison speak, she became a radical abolitionist and practiced "non-resistance" in opposition to slavery, which included a refusal to vote, to become a jury member, or to join the military. She became a lecturer and fundraiser for the Anti-Slavery Society, and, with her husband, Stephen Symonds Foster, provided shelter for fugitive slaves on their Worcester farm.

Francis Jackson, 1789–1861, who was born in Newton, Massachusetts, was an active public figure in Boston, a member of the Boston City Council, and a member of various commissions. Manager of the South Cove Commission, he oversaw the expansion of Boston by 77 filled acres. He was an active abolitionist and a member of various anti-slavery societies, including the Massachusetts Anti-Slavery Society. Jackson was an early supporter and mentor to Frederick Douglass on his arrival in Massachusetts and provided refuge at his Boston home for fugitive slaves.

## Music

John Wallace Hutchinson, 1821–1908, of New Hampshire, brought his family together as the Hutchinson Family Singers to form the most popular four-part singing group in the United States in the 1840s. They began singing at temperance events, then joined abolitionist rallies and events, and wrote abolitionist songs in 1843. Their most popular song, "Get off the Track," was first sung in 1844, two months before the August 2 rally in Hingham.

John, Judson, Asa, Abby, and Jesse Hutchinson participated in the Tranquility Grove rally, came by steamboat from Boston, and were marooned overnight on the way back to Boston with several hundred others. In 1845, they joined Frederick Douglass on a lecture tour of England. John's published journal included colorful accounts of the great abolitionist picnic, and of the Boston Harbor stranding overnight.

Almira Seymour of Hingham wrote a poem and song for the Hingham Anti-Slavery Pic Nic, which was sung by Nathan Lincoln and later published in the *Hingham Patriot*. She also contributed songs to Jairus Lincoln's *Anti-Slavery Melodies*. In Hingham history, she was known both as a teacher in Boston, and as a writer of hymns and poems "which entitle her to be numbered among the women poets of the century."

The Hingham Anti-Slavery Choir performed songs from Jairus Lincoln's *Anti-Slavery Melodies*, which he had arranged and published in 1843 in anticipation of the August 1 celebrations. Paula Bagger of the Hingham Historical Society has noted: "Lincoln

Stephen Symonds Foster. (*Collection of the Massachusetts Historical Society*)

Abby Kelley. (*Collection of the Massachusetts Historical Society*)

Hutchinson Family Singers.

included the words and music to 57 anti-slavery songs, some original, some 'standards' in the movement, and some taken from a previous anthology, *The Anti-Slavery Pick-nick.* Many of the melodies are based on hymns that would have been very familiar to the audience, with lyrics based on anti-slavery poetry by John Pierpont, Elizabeth Margaret Chandler, John Greenleaf Whittier, and Henry Wadsworth Longfellow, among others." Lincoln had encouraged the use of music in rallies and wrote: "There are many who have not the gift of speech-making, but who can, by song-singing, make strong appeals, in behalf of the slave, to every community and every heart."

## Committee of Arrangements

Jairus Lincoln, Chief Marshal for the West India Celebration, also worked with a Committee of Arrangements who coordinated the events of the day, setting up Tranquility Grove for the Pic Nic, organizing the procession and meeting places, inviting contributions of food, and placing articles and posters throughout the region. This was in addition to his *Anti-Slavery Melodies* songbook, assembled for this event. Jairus Lincoln was active in the Town of Hingham, as a teacher and on various committees. He married Mary Cotton Ware in 1818 in Cambridge. He was born in Boston, and Mary had been born in Hingham. Mary was the daughter of Rev. Henry Ware, minister to the First Church in Hingham for eighteen years, who moved to become the fourth Hollis Professor of Divinity at Harvard College, where he established a program that would become the Harvard Divinity School. His appointment was controversial in the eyes of clergy and laymen who believed him too liberal for the position. He became acting President of Harvard twice.

Anna Quincy Thaxter (1796–1878), of Hingham, had approached her cousin, John Quincy Adams, during the summer of 1843 to come to Hingham to participate in the Pic Nic and "celebration of the first of August." She was one of three Thaxter sisters who were early abolitionists and members of the Third Congregational Society (New North Church). As members of the Hingham Committee on Arrangements for the August 1st celebrations in 1844, their home became a key staging area for the Pic Nic, where neighbors and friends brought food in abundance. Advertisements in the Hingham Patriot announced Committee meetings, Pic Nic details, and information about where goods could be dropped off. Their home was well positioned on North Street, next to the old Methodist Church, down the hill from the Hersey Street entrance to Tranquility Grove.

In addition to her work with the Committee of Arrangements for the August 1 Pic Nic, she participated in anti-slavery fairs and projects. In particular, she was a contributor to *The Liberty Bell*, an annual collection of poems and reflections published by the Friends of Freedom for the Massachusetts Anti-Slavery Fair. In 1845, she wrote "Purity of Heart," including the words, "Abolitionists! may our—high endeavor be an inward light, to keep the path before **us** always bright."

According to the accounts of the day, every corner of the Town of Hingham was festooned for the great Anti-Slavery Pic Nic and rally. Bells rang at dawn, noon, and eve. Stores were decorated. Flags lined the streets, and banners were strung across the roads and paths, in addition to those in Tranquility Grove.

There was no mention of cleanup after the events, so one must assume the hard-working committee continued its duties for some time to come.

Lucretia Leonard, 1818–1904. Anna and her sisters, Catherine and Eliza, employed a black servant, Lucretia Leonard, who was born in 1818. Lucretia's mother, Margaret Calley Leonard, moved from Pembroke to Marshfield, where she married John Quacum. After he died, she married James Tuttle of Hingham in 1832, and Lucretia Leonard became his step-daughter. When she worked for the Thaxter sisters, she would accompany them to church on Sundays, and would sit alone in the segregated upper church "slave galleries."

In 1840, the sisters worked with the new pastor at the Third Congregational Society, the Reverend Oliver Stearns, to call for the end of segregation with the Plymouth County Anti-Slavery Society. They invited Lucretia to join them in their family pew, in spite of complaints by other members of the congregation. She sat in the family pew each Sunday, took care of and outlived her employers, and passed away in 1904. Lucretia Leonard is buried in the Hingham Cemetery next to the Thaxter sisters.

Hingham abolitionists Anna Quincy Thaxter and her sisters who were key members of the 1844 Tranquility Grove events are buried together in the Hingham Cemetery, next to Lucretia Leonard.

Lucretia Leonard. (*Collection of Hingham Historical Society*)

# 5

# Other Hingham Abolitionists

*Not All is Changed*, Hingham's most recent written history, provides a chronicle of the early abolitionist activities in the town. The Hingham Anti-Slavery Committee was established by women in 1835. They were affiliated with First Baptist Church. Correspondence available through the Boston Public Library describes Hingham visits of Angelina Grimke (1805–1879), and of Frederick Douglass in the early 1840s. Letters to and from the Weston sisters of Weymouth and Boston discussed anti-slavery fairs and picnics, which were scheduled to raise funds for abolitionist and Underground Railroad efforts.

Several abolitionists who did not attend the Pic Nic of August 2, 1844 were, nonetheless, central to the event and to the work of the abolitionists.

## Sydney Howard Gay

Although there is no record of his having participated in any of the Massachusetts West India Emancipation Celebration events of 1844, Sarah H. Southwick includes in her *Reminiscences of Early-Slavery Days* her memory that the abolitionists went on their "annual picnic ... at the suggestion of Mr. Sydney Howard Gay [1814–1888], whose home was in Hingham, to a very beautiful grove." Gay grew up on South Street in Hingham, about a mile from the grove.

This key abolitionist figure was a member of Hingham's Gay family. Born in Hingham, Sydney Howard Gay attended Derby Academy and Harvard College. His father, Ebenezer Gay, an attorney, hoped that Sydney would join him in his practice. Instead, he drifted in and out of Harvard, and into the China trade, before finding a cause to motivate him.

His strong radical abolitionist early years are thoroughly described in one Hingham history, which wrote: "Debarred from pursuing his chosen profession, that of the law, from his unwillingness to take the oath supporting a Constitution which recognized slavery, he threw himself with enthusiasm, while still young, into the anti-slavery cause

*Right:* Sydney Howard Gay. (*Collection of Massachusetts Historical Society*)

*Below:* Sydney Howard Gay Home on South Street in Hingham.

under the leadership of Garrison." The Hingham history continued, mentioning his distinguished ancestors: "Mr. Gay came naturally by his radical turn of thought, by his independence, courage, strong moral convictions, and good fighting qualities; for in his veins ran the blood of John Cotton and the Mathers, Nehemiah Walter and Ebenezer Gay, among the divines of Colonial New England, and Governor Bradford and James Otis among those who shaped her political fortunes." Gay wrote, toward the end of his life "My ancestry is the best part of me."

When Gay became committed to abolitionist principles, he joined William Lloyd Garrison and offered his services. Gay worked with Garrison and the "Boston clique" on the abolitionist lecture circuit before moving to New York. He became a "lecturing-agent" of the American Anti-Slavery Society from 1843–44, and then editor of the Society's *National Anti-Slavery Standard* in New York from 1844–58, following in the footsteps of the distinguished abolitionist Lydia Maria Child who with her husband had founded the journal. The *National Anti-Slavery Standard* was a sister journal to Garrison's *The Liberator*.

There was reference in the *Standard* to Hingham's August First West India celebrations. One summary report cited the *National Anti-Slavery Standard*, reporting that the August 1 celebrations at Tranquility Grove began with "nine cheers and a prayer."

In later years, Gay became managing editor of the *New York Tribune* and of the *Chicago Tribune*, and wrote and participated in the writing of histories.

Gay's chronicle of the circumstances of fugitive slaves using the Underground Railroad was discovered in Columbia University archives in recent years, and two new books have been published that draw from his meticulous records. The Boston clique, including Gay, not only wrote and published anti-slavery articles and ran events, but also provided stations where fugitive slaves could be welcomed and passed along to their next destinations. The *National Anti-Slavery Standard* was an important journal, as well as an important station on the Underground Railroad in the rescue of slaves escaping to New England and to New York and Canada.

Columbia University History Professor Eric Foner, the author of *Gateway to Freedom: The Hidden History of the Underground Railroad*, wrote that Gay's records were discovered by Madeline Lewis, an undergraduate at Columbia who was working on a senior thesis. Located in some eighty boxes of Gay's records were two journals that chronicled the journeys of slaves to freedom. Foner began his book research based on Gay's journals. These journals include mention of meetings with Harriet Tubman, the legendary "General" on the Underground Railroad, who crossed the Mason-Dixon Line repeatedly to bring out groups of those who were enslaved.

In 1878, Gay published William Jennings Bryan's *Popular History of the United States*, after Bryan's death. Gay is buried with his wife and family in the Hingham Cemetery.

Sarah Southwick's long description of the day and of Sydney Howard Gay included the story of the overnight stranding of the steamer departing Hingham after the Pic Nic. Although the marooning was the subject of great mirth after the fact, thereafter Miss Southwick avoided the steamboat and took the train to a grove in Abington to celebrate West India Celebration days. She may well have participated in a railroad excursion to August 1 anti-slavery celebrations in a "Beautiful Grove" in Framingham in 1853, which featured many of the same speakers who appeared in Tranquility Grove in 1844.

Sydney Howard Gay's record of March 17 and March 20, 1856 of the paths of escape of those fleeing slavery. (*Collection of Columbia University Libraries*)

A broadside advertising August 1 celebrations in Framingham in 1853 included a railroad excursion.

## Rev. Samuel J. May

Rev. Samuel J. May (1797–1871) was Minister of the Second Parish in Scituate and is mentioned in a historical roster of Hingham speech makers. He delivered a sermon in the Third Congregational Church (New North Church) in 1837 at the time of the death of Mrs. Cecilia Brooks, wife of the Rev. Charles Brooks, who was then Pastor of the Third Congregational Society in Hingham. Mr. and Mrs. Brooks had been friends of Abigail May Alcott, Samuel May's sister, who had visited with them in 1828, when she was engaged in her courtship with Bronson Alcott.

Samuel May was an important member of the Garrison group and became a key figure in the Underground Railroad, sheltering thousands of fugitive slaves and helping them move on to Canada after he transferred to the Syracuse area of New York. He appeared in abolitionist rallies and gatherings and had participated as a speaker in Concord on August 1, 1844. May was among the earliest to call for celebrations to mark the August 1 date of the emancipation of slaves in the West Indies.

There is no mention of where he might have been on August 2, and there is no record of his having participated in the Hingham events that day. Since he did share the podium in Concord on August 1 with Ralph Waldo Emerson and Frederick Douglass, he may well have joined the Hingham events.

May's records are stored in the Samuel J. May Anti-Slavery Collection at Cornell and offer significant resources for those studying abolitionists and the Underground Railroad.

Rev. Samuel Joseph May in 1847.
(*Collection of Massachusetts Historical Society*)

## Albert Fearing

Albert Fearing (1798–1875) grew up and lived in Hingham and established a fortune in ship chandlery and manufacturing. He was a philanthropist who founded the Hingham Library. Fearing was also a leader in the American Colonization Society (ACS), which advocated returning blacks to Africa, and eventually became its President. He was elected a state senator and was generally active in politics.

In a speech given in 2012, David J. Mehegan, Chairman of the Hingham Public Library Board of Trustees, noted that Fearing was "strongly anti-slavery," that he had purchased the freedom of twenty slaves from Tennessee, and had helped "finance their emigration to Liberia." Others in Hingham in the 1840s, such as the Rev. Charles Brooks of the Third Congregational Society (New North Church), were also active in the American Colonization Society.

Fearing donated $30,000, a huge sum in those days, for the establishment of the Hingham Library and another $30,000 to the Treasury of the Trustees of Donations for Education in Liberia, Liberia College. Albert Fearing was a member of the Board of Liberia College and President of the Board of Trustees. The American Colonization Society was supported by abolitionists, black freedmen, and slaveholders who believed the presence of free blacks in the United States to be a negative influence. It was opposed strongly by other blacks and abolitionists, who believed that blacks would and should eventually be integrated into white society, including Frederick Douglass. A number of presidents of the ACS were Southerners. The society and the colonization effort in Africa has been seen as both anti-slavery and pro-slavery by historians over the years.

## Maria Weston Chapman

Originally from Weymouth, where her family owned property used for abolitionist rallies, including one portrayed in the Susan Torrey Merritt's 1845 collage of the abolitionist picnic in Weymouth Landing, Maria Weston Chapman (1806–1885) was an ally of William Lloyd Garrison in his "Boston clique," helped him edit *The Liberator*, and lived nearby in Boston with her family.

A powerful and strong-minded individual, she was active in and on the Boards of anti-slavery societies, a co-founder of the Boston Anti-Slavery Society in 1832, ran anti-slavery fairs and procured unique goods for these from Europe as well as the United States, and published *The Liberty Bell*, an annual collection of anti-slavery poetry and writing sold as a fundraiser at the annual Boston Anti-Slavery Bazaar. Chapman ran the Bazaar for almost twenty-five years. She corresponded with many abolitionists, including those in Hingham, and wrote a number of books and publications. The women with whom she worked were often the earliest to organize in their communities to raise money for the causes supported by the abolitionists. Maria Weston Chapman was not from Hingham, but was a significant correspondent and motivator of these events.

*Above left:* Albert Fearing, who was President of the American Colonialization Society. (*Collection of the Hingham Historical Society*)

*Above right:* Maria Weston Chapman was one of the most powerful figures among the Boston abolitionists. (*Collection of Massachusetts Historical Society*)

Albert Fearing lived on North Street in Hingham, in the residence which is now the rectory of St. Paul Church.

# 6

# Groves and Tranquility Grove

## Groves in History

Communing with nature in groves of trees and meadows has been part of human nature since the beginning of time. These have been places for church and family picnics, for speeches and celebrations, for reaching out to the poetic muse, for walking and simple enjoyment, for refreshment of the soul, and for reveling in the spring. There have been countless sacred groves, dedicated to special ritual purposes or limited to a few. Where cities were dirty underfoot, with air foul from pollution, and streets littered with debris, retreating to groves in the country was seen as beneficial to health as well.

Groves have long been celebrated in song and poetry. A madrigal by Henry Purcell (1659–1695), which is still performed, declares: "In these delightful, pleasant groves, let us celebrate our happy happy loves. Let us pipe, pipe and dance. And revel in the happy happy Spring."

## The Alcotts and Tranquility Grove

Tranquility Grove, or Tranquillity Grove, was an important part of the Hingham scene for at least twenty years before the great gathering of 1844. In her journal, Abigail May mused about the delight of walking at night through the Grove. She had arrived in Hingham on August 20, 1828 by packet from Boston to visit her friends the Rev. Charles Brooks of New North Church and his wife, Cecilia. On Friday, August 22, she wrote:

> *Friday, August 22nd*. Passed the evening at Tranquillity Grove. What magic moonlight throws over everything. The most indifferent objects assume a light or shade that gives them interest.

May then wrote in her journal an excerpt of a poem by a contemporary English poet John Bowring:

> *A holy stillness fills the sky,*
> *While evening tunes its vesper song,*
> *And like a sacred lamp on high*
> *The solitary moon is hung.*

It was a time of romance and courtship for her. In his later years, in 1881, Abigail's husband, Bronson Alcott, wrote about his pleasant Hingham memories and "sweet love's symposium" in a sonnet.

> *Hither, the gray and shapely church beside,*
> *At sandy Hingham, by the sounding sea,*
> *From the disturbing town escaped thus wide,*
> *I'm come, from all encumbering care set free,*
> *To raise the choral song, with friends discourse,*
> *Roam the wide fields for flowers, or seaward sail,*
> *Or to Cohasset's strand repair, where hoarse*
> *Tumultuous surges chant their ceaseless tale;*
> *Or poesy entertain, grave Wordsworth's lays,*
> *Melodious musing childhood's glorious prime*
> *Shakespeare's warm sonnets or Venetian plays,*
> *Or that sad wizard Mariner's marvelous Rime.*
> *Here in these haunts, this lovers' company*
> *Sweet Love's symposium hold we happily.*

The ritual or sacred element of groves may explain the wearing of white and the parading of branches and fronds of leaves in processions like the one pictured below, from a Boston Public Library mural. Signaling innocence or virginity, representing the spirit or air, freshness, and perhaps even the fashion of the day, wearing white has classical antecedents. Women wearing white in processionals, bedecked with floral garlands, are still seen today at women's colleges in their favorite festival traditions. Women's rights marchers wear the white of their earlier suffragette sisters, whose white denoted purity. The white of today's marchers represents rebellion and equality. Much is made of the women in the Legion of Honor wearing white and carrying garlands of leaves in the procession to Tranquility Grove on August 2, 1844.

## Other Hingham Groves

Several other Hingham groves mentioned in the newspapers of 1844 included the Eel River Woods, a grove off Water Street, and the "forest sanctuary" at the top of Baker Hill. A grove located to the southeast of the Old Colony House near today's Nantasket Junction commuter rail station, and the steamboat landing, was another. Today, a peaceful grassy treed area next to the Hingham bathing beach and overlooking Hingham Harbor is called simply, "The Grove." Several picnic tables and benches welcome family gatherings during the summer, in particular.

*Left:* An ancient procession of mythic women robed in white and carrying branches in homage. This image is from a mural, "The Muses of Inspiration hail the Spirit, The Messenger of Light," by French artist Pierre Puvis de Chavannes in the Boston Public Library.

*Below:* The Grove overlooking Hingham Harbor today.

In late September 1844, temperance forces gathered for a "Cold Water Army Pic Nic." This too involved a parade and dozens of banners, starting at the Baptist Meeting House and proceeding down Water Street to a Grove behind Captain Calvin Gardiner's residence. According to the *Hingham Patriot* of September 20, 1844: "Here a good deal of labor had been bestowed in clearing up the leaves, trimming the trees, arranging the tables, etc. Just at the entrance of the grove or thicket was a beautiful arch under which the army defiled, and on either side were tables covered with a profusion of cakes, fruits, etc., tastefully arranged with bouquets of flowers."

A month before, a Temperance Society Pic Nic was held at Gill's Lot as an alternative to the Eel River Grove. The procession included a band, banners, and "bright and happy faces." The Gill's Lot grove was described in the *Hingham Patriot* as "just the best place that could be found. A grove of fine large pines, the ground rising on three sides from the area in the middle, and carpeted thick with dried leaves which had fallen from the trees."

Celebration Pic Nics and events marking West Indian Emancipation Day, a tradition that began in the 1840s, were held in groves, in churches, and in public buildings. In 1843, an August 1 celebration took place in Weymouth. Susan Torrey Merritt's college "Antislavery Picnic at Weymouth Landing, Massachusetts" may well have been a representation of this event. The property, as mentioned earlier, was owned by the Weston family, Weymouth abolitionists. Weymouth also offered a popular grove at Lovell's Landing, located on the Fore River. It is now the location of an energy plant (decidedly not bucolic), at a point of land which was then accessible from Boston by ferry.

This famous collage, created by Susan Torrey Merritt of Weymouth, portrays an anti-slavery picnic in Weymouth Landing. Dated 1845, it may illustrate an 1843 August 1 celebration. It is one of the most highly regarded pieces of folk painting in the United States. (*Courtesy of the Art Institute of Chicago*)

In 1844, when several Massachusetts communities made plans to host festivities to commemorate the tenth anniversary of the August 1 Emancipation of Slavery in the West Indies, they included New Bedford, the destination of many fugitive slaves, including Frederick Douglass; a group of Boston's black churches; Concord; and Hingham. Other groves and locations were also suggested.

One proposal, published on June 21, came from a gentleman in Dorchester who suggested Tenean Grove overlooking Boston Harbor in Dorchester as a potential location for the August 1 anti-slavery picnic. The gentleman pointed out that participants from Hingham could take a steamboat and land off Commercial Point, "a short distance from the Grove." But Hingham had already been organized under the leadership of Jairus Lincoln and his active committee. Notice was posted in *The Liberator* on June 26 about the "Union Celebration of the 1st of August" for the event in Hingham.

## Tranquility Grove

The annual report of the Hingham Anti-Slavery Society for 1844 included a summary description of the Tranquility Grove event, which appeared in the *Hingham Patriot* in January 24, 1845. It surrounds the event in the grove with a sense of the sacred as well as the secular:

> At the solicitation of our Anti-Slavery friends in the neighboring counties, we united with them in the commemoration of W. I. Emancipation on the 1st of August in Tranquility Grove. That occasion will long be remembered in the annals of Massachusetts Anti-Slavery. Its marshaled hosts, its array of music and banners, and the solemn and affecting sublimity of the scene, when thousands stood uncovered in that "temple not made with hands," while the fervent prayer of Thanksgiving and contrition ascended to the God of love and mercy; all these circumstances are yet green in memory, and need not be recounted. The influence of that day is among the imperishable things of the spirit.

Described as being about 25 acres, located between today's Central Street, Hersey Street, and Elm Street, Tranquility Grove was owned by Edward Thaxter and Henry Thaxter. The grove was accessible from various paths, including what was to be the main parade route adjacent to Henry Thaxter's house, "Tranquility Lodge" at 137 Main Street.

Marian Studley, writing in 1943 about "An 'August First' in 1844," a century earlier, exclaimed "it seems as if this grove were made by the hand of Nature for the purpose to which it is this day to be put."

The thousands who arrived for the celebration of West Indian Emancipation on August 2 came by coach and ferry from Norfolk, Plymouth, Suffolk, and Essex counties. As described, they paraded into Tranquility Grove, which had been set forth with an array of food, listened to a day of speeches, and enjoyed the food and hospitality of the women of Hingham and those from Boston.

Unfortunately, great damage was done to the grove from the August 2 celebrations, to the extent that the Thaxters decided to end the public use of the grove. *Not All is Changed*, Hingham's most recent history, published in 1993, documents the damage, reported in the *Hingham Patriot* in 1850. "Brothers Edward and Henry Thaxter," the owners, found that the "mass gathering … had ravaged and almost ruined the choice retreat."

Evidence of this appeared in the *Hingham Patriot* when a poet in the congregation of the Universalist Church printed an ode that bemoaned the loss of Tranquility Grove for their annual picnic, and the cutting of the trees in the grove. The Universalist Church found a new home for its picnic in a forest grove atop Baker's Hill.

From the *Hingham Patriot*, September 6, 1844, here is an excerpt of the poem, which appears in the Appendix in full:

> *Where shall our Festival be held?*
> *Mammon our forest fane has felled!*
> *His iron hand has bared the soil—*
> *God's temple his unholy spoil.…*
> *That place of justice, where the word*
> *Was uttered, that deep hearts has stirred,*
> *When pressing thousands gathered round,*
> *To catch of* Freedom's' *voice the sound,*
> *Freedom from chains of sin and sense,*
> *And tyrany's omnipotence—…*
> *Where were ye, Nymphs of tree and dell,*
> *When on your home destruction fell?*
> *When the reverberating stroke*
> *First on your startled senses broke?…*
> *But while I mourn, and mourn in vain,*
> *That plaintive voice is heard again—*
> *"Where shall our festival be held?"*
> *"Despair not—though we are expelled*
> *"From this so loved, so fair retreat,*
> *"…And though no spot can ever be*
> *To them what was* Tranquillity
> *Long shall they cherish fondly still,*
> *The Pic Nic upon* Baker's Hill.
> *August, 1844.*

## Tranquility Grove Since 1844

After the great abolitionist picnic, Tranquility Grove faded into memory, although there was reference in 1844 to a gathering in the grove after the events of August 2. *Not All is Changed* described a "sylvan baptism" in Tranquility Grove in 1850, which brought together for the first time in forty-four years the congregations of New North Church, led by Reverend Oliver Stearns, and First Parish (Old Ship Church) led by Reverend Joseph Richardson.

The part of the property owned by Edward Thaxter was eventually divided on July 3, 1849. In a Supreme Court decision dated January 4, 1879, *Peters vs. Siders*, 126 Mass. 135, the division of the property was discussed.

The plaintiff, Edward Dyer Peters, sued to recover land that had belonged to his mother, Susan Thaxter Peters, which included "an undivided half of certain land commonly known as the 'Tranquility Grove Lot' in Hingham, in addition to ten acres of pasture land located on both sides of Central Street." She had left her entire estate to her husband, without provision for her child, in a will dated a month after Edward's birth. The plaintiff was unsuccessful in his suit, and the land remained with Mr. Siders, to whom Henry H. Peters, the father of the plaintiff, had sold the property in 1864 and 1868.

A portion of the Thaxter property remains as the Burns Memorial Park, now owned by the Hingham Conservation Commission, and accessible by a walkway near the intersection of Elm and Hersey Streets. The property of 24.1 acres is overgrown with brush and briars. The last chapter outlines possible options for restoring the Park as an attractive grove and open space, and as an educational opportunity providing an important story about an important moment in local history.

# 7

# Tranquility Lodge and Roseneath Cottage

Two houses, "Tranquility Lodge" and "Roseneath Cottage," built on the property that provided the access to Tranquility Grove, are part of Hingham town history. The right of way to Tranquility Grove was on Henry Thaxter's property. The following section describes what happened to that right of way.

## Tranquility Lodge and the Right of Way

Former Hingham resident Kate Dickerson, who lived in Tranquility Lodge which is still located at 137 Main Street on Bachelor's Row in the Lincoln Historic District, provided notes and historic background for this property. Owned by Henry Thaxter in 1844, a right of way immediately adjacent to the house (still marked by granite posts) was identified in the *Hingham Patriot* as the entry point for the August First procession to Tranquility Grove. Henry Thaxter and his brother Edward Thaxter, who lived next door, owned Tranquility Grove.

Dickerson, who lived in the house from 1985 to 2010, pointed out the granite posts still located immediately to the right of 137 Main Street: "There was a driveway along the West side of the property, which ran back to Roseneath Cottage. Two large granite posts, with iron hardware for a gate, flank what used to be the driveway to Roseneath Cottage, on the West side of the house. The legal easement for this driveway became void after years of disuse, and the former driveway is now fully part of the Tranquility Lodge property, with no legal encumberments." After the Roseneath property was separated from Tranquility Lodge and new bounds were established, the use of the right of way was abandoned, Dickerson said.

On the "Plan of the Susan B. Willard Estate of December 31, 1936," the right of way from Main Street to Susan Willard's property (owned by the Hingham Historical Society) was shown to be "8 feet wide" and slightly over 145 feet long (see Plan 1).

The right of way that eventually became part of the property at 137 Main Street was no longer shown on the 1969 plan prepared for Lucius P. Davis, two years after

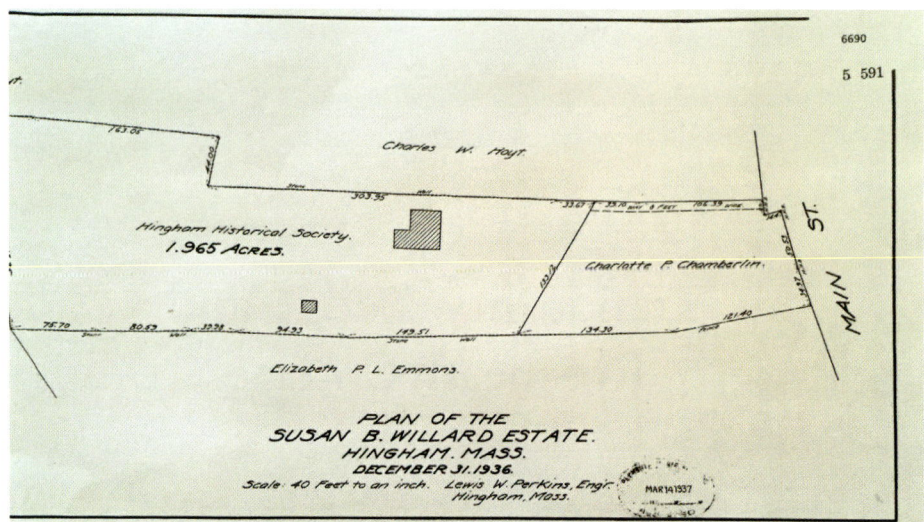

*Above:* Plan 1 showing the easement of the old Thaxter property, allowing access from Main Street to Central Street.

*Below:* Plan 2 showing the abandonment of the easement, and the elimination of access between Main Street and Central Street.

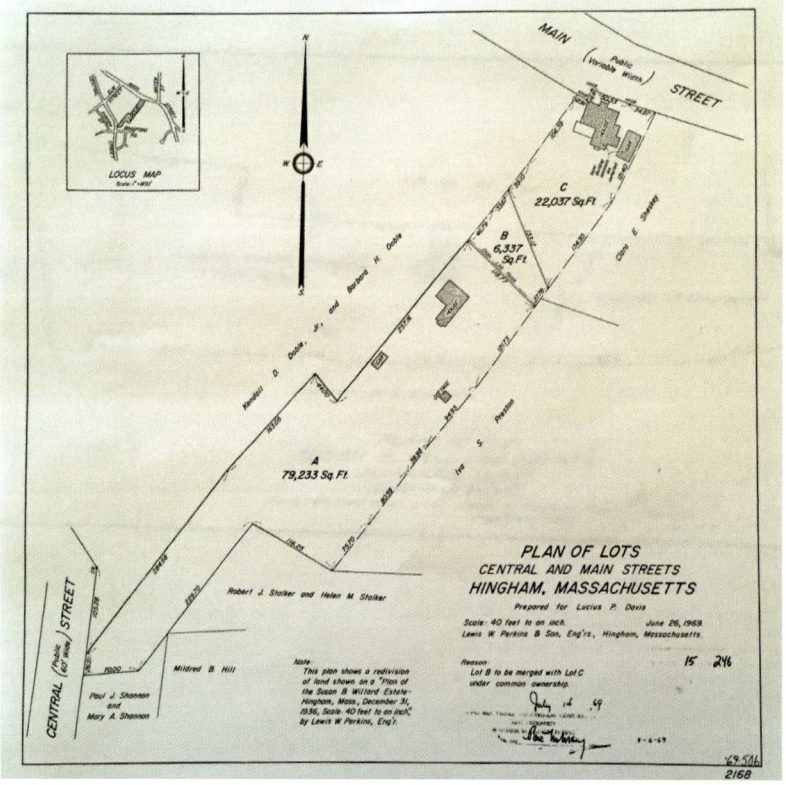

he and Katherine Davis purchased the Roseneath Cottage property from the Hingham Historical Society on April 30, 1967.

In the original deed, Davis purchased the entire Susan Willard estate parcel from the Historical Society, including some 6,337 square feet that abutted the easement on Main Street. The 1969 plan shows the 6,337 square foot piece of the Willard/Historical Society property was to be transferred or sold to the Main Street property. A "chain link fence" is shown on the plan dividing the Main Street and Central Street properties, indicating a firm separation of the properties (see Plan 2).

The granite posts marking the old right of way, which were recently exposed because of construction and landscaping work, can still be seen behind the fence at 137 Main Street.

The photo below shows one of the granite posts marking the old right of way (to the left and slightly behind the center wooden telephone pole) as well as the homes of Henry and Edward Thaxter, who jointly owned Tranquility Grove in 1844. One could assume that both adjacent rights of way provided the August 1 West India Celebration access for the procession, although only Henry Thaxter's property was mentioned in the *Hingham Patriot* announcement in July, 1844.

According to Kate Dickerson, Tranquility Lodge was a name attached to the house "since at least the mid-1800s." She added: "... one report says it [the name] is as old

Granite posts marking one side of the walkway from Main Street to Tranquility Grove can be seen between 135 and 137 Main Street. Tranquility Lodge is to the left, and its granite posts are still there, behind the fence.

as the house. It got its name from the old acreage behind the house which was called Tranquility Grove, and was famous for pre-revolutionary political gatherings, and again later for stirring abolitionist meetings."

The house was built in 1709 by Sarah James, on land granted to Thomas Thaxter in 1637. The house was rebuilt in 1767 by Jotham Loring. According to Dickerson: "... the house stayed in the same 'family' through inheritance and marriage, until 1920."

Dickerson noted that the Tranquility Lodge property had "extended back to Central Street, which abutted Tranquility Grove." She also pointed out that "Tranquility" was also spelled as "Tranquillity," and wrote: "... so both spellings are correct."

Henry Thaxter left his mark in the house: "One of the windowpanes in the front west bedroom is inscribed H. T. Thaxter [probably with a diamond, as was often done]. Henry Thaxter, who married Jotham Loring's sister, owned the house from 1788."

## Roseneath Cottage

Roseneath Cottage, also still standing, and located on part of the Tranquility Lodge property, originally held a driveway easement that extended between Main Street and Central Street "at least through the life of Susan Barker Willard," according to Dickerson. The cottage address was listed as 135 Main Street through 1970.

An early view of Roseneath Cottage. The small house was moved several times, ending up on the back property at 137 Main Street. It is now accessible from Central Street, since the property bounds were changed. The sale of Roseneath Cottage endowed the creation of the Hingham Historical Society.

The cottage itself has a long history. An article published by the Daughters of the American Revolution in 1911 and a later article in *Good Housekeeping* describe the building's legends. Some have said that the cottage, which was moved three times, was constructed before 1681. Known as the George Hayward house when she purchased it, and the Benjamin Lane-Enoch Lane house earlier, Susan Willard moved the cottage to the family property behind Tranquility Lodge in 1903.

Susan Willard was living in Roseneath Cottage at the time of her death in 1926 and willed the property to the Hingham Historical Society, as well as all her "furniture, furnishings, china, portraits and pictures," with some exceptions. The property was owned by the Hingham Historical Society and rented out through at least 1967, according to deeds recorded by Julian Loring. The Hingham Historical Society voted to sell the property on April 30, 1967. The address was changed in 1970 from 135 Main Street to 102 Central Street, since the Main Street right of way was eliminated in 1969. Roseneath Cottage is currently owned by Hingham residents James and Rosalie Macella.


## Susan Barker Willard

Kate Dickerson described Susan Barker Willard in her notes as "the most famous resident of Tranquility Lodge, who acquired the house in 1894." Willard was one of the founders of the Hingham Historical Society, of the local branch of the Daughters of the American Revolution, of the Village Improvement Society, and the local chapter of the Arts and Crafts Movement. The Arts and Crafts Movement was a branch of the movement founded in England by William Morris and his associates in 1901. Dickerson describes old photos of Miss Willard and members of the Arts and Crafts group meeting in a living room of her house. Willard was also a proponent of public education, "especially for children." She founded a kindergarten, held in her home, Tranquility Lodge. During her residence in this larger house, Susan Barker Willard used her home for social and political gatherings, "as it had been throughout its history."

Susan Barker Willard left Roseneath Cottage to the Hingham Historical Society in her will, as well as its furnishings and possessions, including five of the original banners which were hung throughout Tranquility Grove on August 2, 1844. Many of the objects were transferred to the Old Ordinary, a former tavern, when it became a museum of the Hingham Historical Society. She was the granddaughter of Francis Barker, who had owned the Old Ordinary. She was also the great-great-granddaughter of early Hingham settler Samuel Thaxter.

Susan Barker Willard, in historic costume, with Roseneath Cottage furnishings and artifacts eventually willed to the Hingham Historical Society, where they can be seen in the Old Ordinary today. (*Collection of Hingham Historical Society*)

# 8

# Tranquility Grove Property

## Tranquility Grove Ownership

How did Tranquility Grove come into being? An early map of Hingham showing historic land divisions indicates that the open areas forming Tranquility Grove were originally given to early settlers Daniel Cushing (lot 56 crossing Hersey Street), Jos. Bates (lot 50, off of Hersey Street), and Josiah Hobart (lot 51, on Hersey Street). The three large lots were bounded at the time by long, narrow house lots to the East and North, and by Hersey Street on the West. Across Hersey Street, large lots owned by Daniel Cushing and Thomas Richards extended to New Bridge Street. The division of the adjacent house lots took place from 1636–1638. There is no date attached to the open lot divisions, though it could have been part of the 6th division. Many of the long lots in Hingham were designated for agriculture.

As mentioned earlier, at the time of the Tranquility Grove events of August 2, 1844, the Grove was owned by Henry Thaxter and Edward Thaxter. In 1848, Edward Thaxter's portion of the property was conveyed to Harry Peters, upon the death of his wife, Susan Thaxter Peters, the daughter of Edward Thaxter. In 1868, Peters sold the property to Charles Siders. His son, Edward, sued unsuccessfully for his interest in the land.

In 1904, a deed was recorded marking the sale of Tranquility Grove by Catherine Siders, the "Conservator of Charles B. Siders" to Michael Burns of Hingham for $1,500. The deed conveyed "a certain tract of land situated in said Hingham, known as Tranquillity Grove, containing nine acres and twenty-seven rods of land more or less.... Also a certain other tract of pasture land ... containing ten acres more or less."

The first parcel was bounded by Hersey Street, and properties formerly belonging to Edward Thaxter. The second parcel was described as "... being all that portion of the premises convened to Charles Siders by Henry H. Peters which lies Westerly of said Central Street."

The Town of Hingham's "Valuation of Real Estate" for 1910 includes the following description of Michael Burns's open land: Land, 8½ acres, Hersey Street; Tranquility Grove, 4½ acres, Hersey Street; and Peter's lot, 15 acres, Central Street. Michael Burns and Margaret Burns also owned adjacent houses, side buildings, and small open lots at the time.

Charles B. Siders, who purchased part
of the Tranquility Grove property
from Edward Thaxter's son-in-law in
1868. Catherine Siders, his widow, sold
Tranquility Grove to Michael Burns in
1904. The Burns Family sold the property
to the Town of Hingham in 1972.
(*Collection of Hingham Historical Society*)

In 1972, descendants of Michael Burns applied to the Building Commissioner and
then to the Board of Appeals to seek a variance from minimum frontage requirements
for Residence District A. The family sought "only 20′ of frontage" for a 19.33-acre
portion of the 24.49 acres, lying between Central, Emerald, Elm and Hersey Streets. The
19.33-acre portion would be sold to the Town of Hingham for conservation purposes.
The variance was granted by the Board of Appeals on April 17, 1972. The Burns family
sold the 19.33-acre property to the Town of Hingham on June 2, 1972, and asked that
the property be called Burns Memorial Park.

## Burns Memorial Park: Tranquility Grove

If one were to search for the remaining acres of Tranquility Grove, without knowing the
exact location, it would be a challenge. Burns Memorial Park, described as a "wilderness
neighborhood park," may be the most obscure parcel of public land in Hingham's
conservation portfolio. The entrance to an overgrown trail is marked by a battered
wooden sign on Hersey Street.

Described briefly on both the Conservation Land Trust Map of 1982, and in the Town
of Hingham, Massachusetts Open Space and Recreation Plan in the Inventory of Lands
of Conservation and Recreation Interest, the Burns Memorial Park of what is now 24.1
acres represents the last publicly-owned piece of what was Tranquility Grove.

A weathered sign and an obscure access mark the path to Tranquility Grove today, now Burns Memorial Park.

Burns Memorial Park is described on the map of town open spaces, published in 1982, as: "Centrally located, the beautiful 24.1 acres encompass pine covered ledges, meadow and red maple swampland which belonged to the Burns family. In Tranquility Grove, outdoor meetings, such as abolition rallies, were once held."

In the Town of Hingham's Open Space and Recreation Plan for 2009–2016, the "Inventory of Lands of Conservation and Recreation Interest" includes the following information: designated as item C-34, Burns Memorial Park (Tranquility Grove) is owned by the Town Conservation Commission, has 24.1 acres, and is zoned as municipal land open space.

A description of the setting follows:

The varied 'wild' terrain is excellent wildlife habitat. Much of the area is fresh water marsh-meadow and red maple swamp, but the northern and western parts have a high ledge, mature pines and ancient individual hard woods. Old Red Cedars are losing the contest for light to faster growing pines and hardwoods. This 'Old Field' species composition indicates that the northern section was once a cleared pasture.

Access is gained off Hersey Street, across from the former Highway barn. It is described: "… difficult to find without an apparent sign, though reportedly has been marked by a

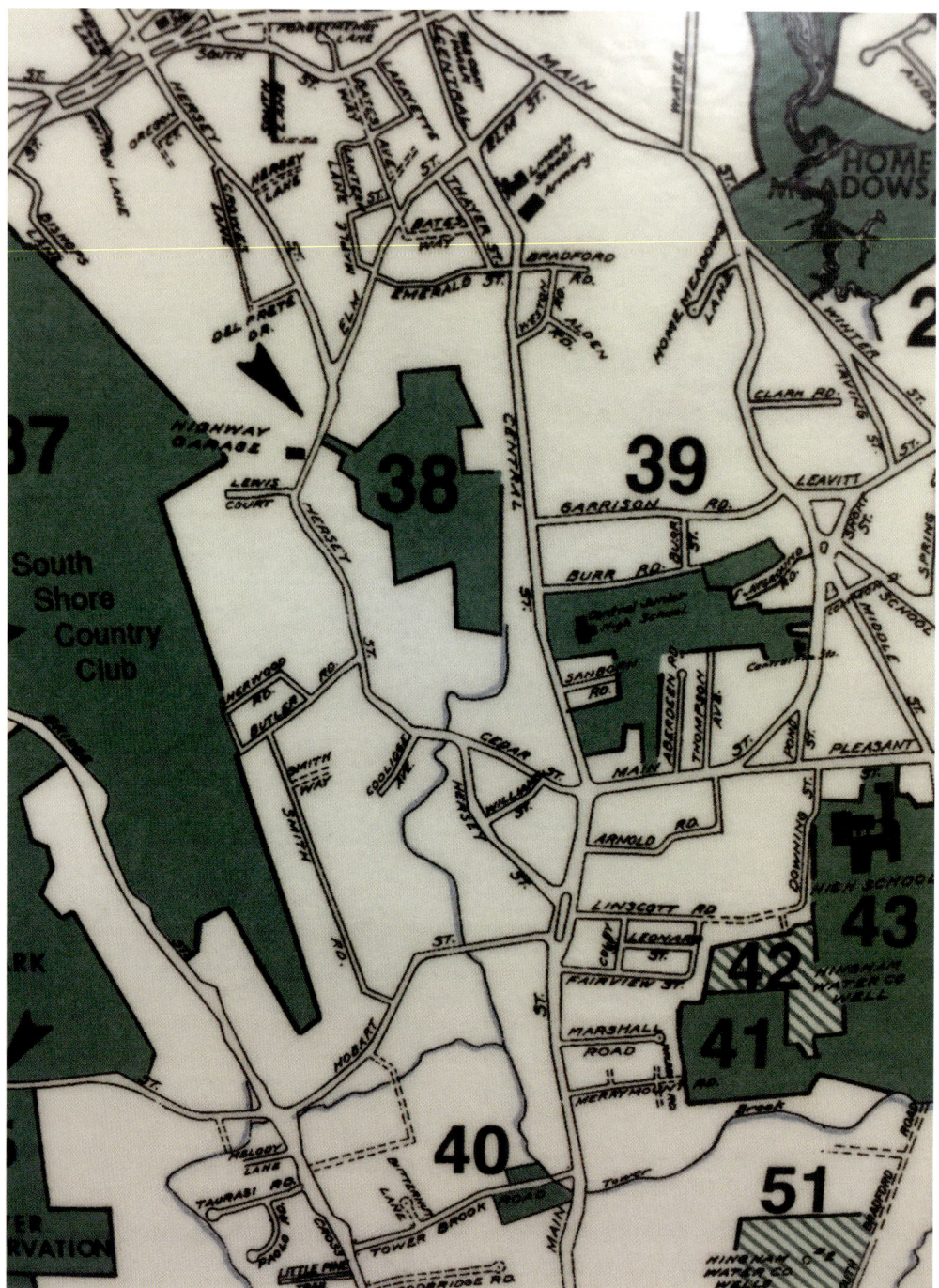

An Open Space and Recreation Plan published by the Hingham Land Trust shows the location of Burns Memorial Park/Tranquility Grove as No. 38, between Hersey Street and Central St. The original right of way into the grove came from Main Street to the right of the Armory. Central Street did not exist in 1844.

large hanging sign." A battered standing sign sits at the entry into the property, and a sign in good condition can be found several hundred feet into the property today.

A description of possible activities suggests "An open space buffer and neighborhood park with definite wildlife value; it allows natural activities such as bird watching and nature photography."

The significance of the property is currently described:

> This gift of Helen Burns is a 'wilderness' neighborhood park. Well-used foot trails show its use by residents whose property backs up to the site from Central, Emerald, Elm and Hersey Streets. Its rugged nature precluded its former use for crops or housing with the happy result that a sizable natural area remains close to Hingham Square.

The open space plan recommends that a connection be created through the woods to nearby Central Street, and suggests improving signage.

Neighbors have reported walking the trail from time to time, and school children over the years used the path for shortcuts to the bus. The pathways were used far more frequently when Central Junior High School was the destination across the grove. That building is now Hingham Town Hall. Today, most sections and trails of what was Tranquility Grove are overgrown with brush. Former Fire Chief Richard Wehter wrote that children used to set fires in the pine grove from time to time. It was a place for

Burns Memorial Park/Tranquility Grove today is a tangle of vines and brush.

middle school and high school boys to hang out. A ghost of a woman wearing white has been seen as well. Occasional ashes and spirits are what remain.

## Reclaiming Tranquility Grove

With the rich trove of information about the significance and uses of Tranquility Grove, including the remarkable and historic abolitionist gathering on August 2, 1844, there is ample information to support both educational and visiting opportunities to the Grove in the future. Examples of abolitionist-themed parks and communities and walking trails abound, as in Florence, Massachusetts, where Sojourner Truth and a utopian group of abolitionists flourished.

In Weymouth Landing, the location of the abolitionist gathering in 1843–45 portrayed on the Susan Merritt Torrey collage was on property owned by the Weston family, including the great abolitionist Maria Weston Chapman. Today there are athletic fields and a library at the location, and a new Maria Weston Chapman School is planned elsewhere in Weymouth.

What are some of the possibilities for Tranquility Grove/Burns Memorial Park? They might include printed materials, interactive media, maps, educational materials, new signs, information kiosks, and walking trails. For instance, an "August 2, 1844 West India Emancipation Celebration Walking Trail" could begin at New North Church (Fountain Square), follow the route of the 1844 procession to Steamboat Wharf, and back to Main Street via. North Street and South Street to 137 Main, and back to Elm Street to reach either the entry of Burns Memorial Park/Tranquillity Grove at Hersey Street, or to a new entrance to Tranquility Grove/Burns Memorial Park somewhere on Central Street. Pieces of the "August 2, 1844" trail could be linked to the new cross-town trail programs underway in the Town of Hingham under the jurisdiction of the Conservation Commission.

Further, considering the significance of Burns Memorial Park/Tranquility Grove to Hingham and Plymouth County history, the Town might consider mapping the details of the park, including the condition of the property, trails, the lay of the land, and the geological and natural features. Exploration of historical easements might identify additional access points to the park, particularly from Central Street. A park cleanup that opens trails and restores "grove" features would be appropriate. (A Spring 2018 tour of the former Tranquility Grove brought Hingham's historical and conservation planners together to think about what the future of the property might be.)

So often in New England, historical societies focus on founding legends, the Pilgrims and Native Americans leading the list, and of events related to the American Revolution. The nineteenth century was a divisive but critically important time in the history of the United States, as the struggle to free slaves and to achieve the goal of equality set forth in the nation's founding documents engaged everyone in different ways. Abolitionists were a minority in our towns, but their goals were eventually achieved in 1863, with Lincoln's issuance of the Emancipation Proclamation, and in 1870, with the ratification of the 15th Amendment. This one event in Tranquility Grove in Hingham, Massachusetts, on August 2, 1844, captures in a day all of the passion, dedication, color, and issues of the time. May it become a new important thread in the historic narrative of the Town of Hingham and the Commonwealth of Massachusetts.

The Sojourner Truth Memorial Park is the starting place for a walking tour of abolitionist homes and locations in Florence, Massachusetts, where she lived and worked.

*Above:* Weymouth Landing location pictured in collage of Susan Torrey Merritt of 1845. Today the former Weston family property is owned by the City of Weymouth, and is the site of the public library and athletic facilities.

*Below:* In the late spring of 2018, members of Hingham's Historical Commission toured Tranquility Grove with the Hingham Conservation Commission and neighbors to assess the conditions of the former Tranquility Grove and to talk about the future.

# Abolitionist Timeline

1641:   Massachusetts legalizes slavery.

1764:   First colonial census reports 77 slaves in Hingham.

1780:   Massachusetts new Constitution adopted, with Declaration of Rights.

1783:   Chief Justice William Cushing decision in Quock Walker case, saying slavery incompatible with Massachusetts Constitution.

1805:   William Lloyd Garrison born, Newburyport.

1828:   Meets Benjamin Lundy, anti-slavery Quaker.

1829:   Delivers anti-slavery address at Park Street Church on Independence Day.

1831:   William Lloyd Garrison founds *The Liberator*, January 1. First issue.

1831:   January 6, 1832, New England Anti-Slavery Society founded with twelve men. Garrison corresponding secretary.

1832:   Writes paper against American Colonialization Society, return of slaves to Africa.

1833:   Formation of American Anti-Slavery Society in Philadelphia.

1833:   Vote in British Parliament to liberate slaves in West Indies.

1833:   Formation of Female Anti-Slavery Society in Boston; disbanded 1840.

1834:   Emancipation of Slaves announced in West Indies, August 1, 1834.

1834:   Formation of Old Colony Anti-Slavery Society.

1835:   Garrison dragged through streets of Boston with a rope around his neck.

1835:   Formation of Hingham Female Anti-Slavery Society.

1838:   Formation of Hingham Anti-Slavery Society.

1837:   Robert Purvis becomes principal organizer of Vigilant Association of Philadelphia, beginning work of Underground Railroad in 1837.

1837:   With the passage of the gag rule in 1828, there was a national effort led by the American Anti-Slavery Society to submit public petitions against slavery. A total of 400,000 came to Congress from throughout the United States during twelve months.

1838:   Former President John Quincy Adams, now Congressman from area, introduced 350 publicly-submitted petitions against slavery in U.S. House of Representatives, violating "gag rule," which forbade introduction of bills dealing with slavery. He linked freedom of petition with the right to free speech. Frederick Douglass flees slavery and goes to New Bedford.

1841: With urging of Dr. Oliver Stearns, segregation was voted down by Plymouth County Anti-Slavery Society; segregation of church came to an end with Thaxter sisters, who invited servant Lucretia Leonard to join them in their pew.

1841: Frederick Douglass speaks in the spring at an anti-slavery meeting in New Bedford, and is invited to speak at a meeting of the Nantucket Anti-Slavery Society on August 11 about his flight from slavery, where he is heard by William Lloyd Garrison. Amazed by his story, Garrison convinces him to become a lecturer for the Massachusetts Anti-Slavery Society.

1841: Frederick Douglass speaks to the quarterly meeting of Plymouth County Anti-Slavery Society at the First Baptist Church in Hingham, November 13, 1841. Reported in the Hingham Patriot. Moderator Samuel J. May.

1842: Samuel J. May encourages celebrations to mark August 1, 1834 emancipation days; fired from pulpit in South Scituate for being outspoken abolitionist.

1843: Sydney Howard Gay of Hingham moves to New York to become editor and publisher of *National Anti-Slavery Standard*.

1843: Plans made for tenth anniversary celebrations of emancipation of slaves in West Indies. Jairus Lincoln collects and publishes Anti-Slavery Melodies, for use of 1844 celebration.

1844: Abolitionist Pic Nic in Hingham's Tranquility Grove, August 2, 1834 (delay because of rain); speeches and parades and celebrations held on August 1 in Concord, Boston, and New Bedford.

1851: Rev. Oliver Stearns delivers sermon opposed to Fugitive Slave Act in Hingham.

1861: Start of Civil War.

1863: Promulgation of Emancipation Proclamation.

1865: End of Civil War.

1870: Ratification of the 15th Amendment to the United States Constitution.

# Appendix

**Letter from John Quincy Adams**
**(as printed in the *Hingham Patriot*)**

The following letter written by John Quincy Adams was read at the Celebration of the West India Emancipation, on August 2, 1844 in Hingham.

Quincy, 29th July, 1844.

Miss Thaxter:

In declining the invitation which I received last summer to attend the celebration of the first of August, it was in no wise my intention to express disapprobation of the celebration itself. The abolition of slavery in the colonies of Great Britain, by the Parliament of that realm, was an event, at which, if the whole human race could have been concentrated in one person, the heart of that person would have leaped for joy. The restoration of 800,000 human beings from a state of degrading oppression to the rights bestowed upon them by the God of nature at their birth, was of itself a cause of rejoicing to the pure in heart throughout the habitable earth. But that is not the only nor the most radiant glory of that day. It was the pledge of Power and of Will of the mightiest nation upon the globe, that the bondage of man shall cease; that the manacle and the fetter shall drop from every limb; that the ties of nature shall no longer be outraged by man's inhumanity to man; that the self-evident truths of our Declaration of Independence shall not longer be idle mockeries, belied by the transcendent power of Slavery, welded into our Constitution. It was the voice of the herald, like that of John the Baptist in the wilderness, proclaiming, as with the trump of the archangel, that the standing fundamental policy of the British Empire was thenceforth the peaceable abolition of slavery throughout the world.

Well, then, may the friends of Freedom and of Man rejoice at the annual return of that day. Well may they, from far and wide, assemble and meet together in mutual gratulation at the return of so blessed a day. Well may they come in crowds to cheer and encourage one another to contribute, every one according to his ability, to the final consummation of this glorious and stupendous undertaking. My unwillingness to participate in it arose only from shame for the honor and good name of my country, whose government, under a false and treacherous pretence of co-operating with Great Britain for the suppression of one of the forms of this execrable system of slavery, has been now for a series of years pursuing and maturing a counteraction of the purpose of Universal Emancipation, and organizing an opposite system for the maintenance, preservation, propagation and perpetuation of slavery throughout the earth.

For the last fifteen years, this unhallowed purpose has been constantly, perseveringly and unblushingly persisted in, with a pertinacity of exertions, and a perfidy in the use of means, never surpassed by any conspiracy ever formed against the liberties of Mankind. The dismemberment of the neighboring republic of Mexico—the re-institution of slavery throughout an immense portion of her territory, and the purchase or conquest of California, with the lying pretension of re-annexing Texas to this Union, have been and yet are among those profligate and unprincipled means; an absurd and preposterous attempt to pick a quarrel with Great Britain upon false and frivolous pretenses, is another. The utter prostration of the exclusive constitutional power of Congress to declare war—the whole compound budget of blunders and of crimes—the abortive negotiation of a Treaty of plunder and robbery, which the Senate had the common sense and common honesty almost unanimously to reject—the glaring falsehoods by which the Texans themselves were inveigled into the negotiation—all these and many more enormities of the deepest dye, are but parts and parcels of the agony of Slavery struggling for existence and perpetuation against the awakening conscience of mankind.

The abortion of slavemongering diplomacy, miscalled a Treaty, attempted in the last hours of an administration detested and despised even by its own partisans, is the last act of this knot of conspirators against human Freedom. Their foul and filthy purpose has at length been extorted from them: It is by an exterminating War to rob Mexico of her provinces and to defend and perpetuate Slavery by open War against England for undertaking to abolish it throughout the world. A self-styled President of the United States, and two successive Secretaries of State of his appointment, have with shameless effrontery avowed, to the scorn and indignation of civilized man, that their project of wholesale treachery, robbery and murder was undertaken and pursued for the deliberate purpose of overreaching, overturning and destroying the system of policy of the British nation to promote the abolition of Slavery throughout the world. I have long foreseen and watched the progress of the two systems towards this issue, and have given formal warning to my countrymen of it, by speeches in the House of Representatives in 1836; 1838; and 1842, by addresses to my constituents in 1837 at Quincy, in 1842 at Braintree, and 1843 at Dedham; and by an address signed by 22 others members of congress and myself, to the People of the Free States at the close of the session of 1843—an address falsely charged by the forty bale weathercock hero of Texan annexation, nullification and the blessings of slavery, as threatening the dissolution of the Union. I have seen the steady and gradual approach of the two systems to the conflict of mortal combat in all their phases, from the strictly confidential Letter of Andrew Jackson of Dec. 10, 1833, to Wm Fulton, Secretary, not Governor, of Arkansas territory, to that consummate device of slavebreeding Democracy, the two-thirds rule of the late Democratic Convention at

Baltimore—and to the casting down of the glove of defiance, by our present Secretary of State, in his Letter to the British Plenipotentiary, Mr. Pakenham, of 18th April last. The glove was indeed not taken up. We are yet to learn with what ears the journal of the trump of slavery was listened to by the British Queen and her ministers. We are yet to learn whether the successor of Elizabeth on the throne of Eland and her Burleighs and Walsinghams, upon hearing that their avowed purpose to promote universal emancipation and the extinction of slavery upon the earth is to be met by the man-robbers of our own country with exterminating War, will, like craven cowards, turn their backs and flee, or eat their own words, or disclaim the purpose which they have avowed. That, Miss Thaxter, is the issue, flung in their faces by President Tyler and his secretary John C. Calhoun. And that is the issue to which they have pledged, to the extent and beyond the extent of their power, you and me, and the free people of this Union, and their posterity, for life and death, for peace and war, for time and eternity.

Shall we respond affirmatively to that pledge? No! by the God of justice and of mercy! No! My heart is full to overflowing; but I have no more room for words. Proceed then to celebrate and solemnize the Emancipation of 800,000 British slaves, whose bonds have been loosened by British hands. Invoke the blessings of Almighty God with prayer that the day may speedily come when the oppressed millions of our own land shall be raised to the dignity and enjoy the rights of Freedom, and when the soil of Texas herself shall be as free as our own. I cannot be with you, for age and infirmity forbid; but for every supplication breathed by you for the universal emancipation of man, and the extinction of slavery upon earth, my voice shall respond Amen!

From your faithful friend and kinsman,

John Quincy Adams

## "Hymn for the 1st of August" by Almira Seymour

A voice o'er the wide blue sea—
  A voice through New-England groves—
A song for the ransomed *Free*,
  Where a crowned head's subjects rove!

A wail from fair Southern plains
  The home of soft airs and flowers—
A wail for the bound with chains,
  In this boasted land of ours!

A shout that the world shall hear—
  A shout that shall reach to Heaven—
Dried up is the captive's tear,
And the captive's bonds are riven.

A cry as from depths below—
A cry as of doomed despair,
For the crushed by Freedom's Foe,

That oppression's burdens bear.
A prayer to the living God—
Thanksgiving and grateful praise,
That England, a tyrant's rod
O'er the Black man cannot raise!

A yearning and pleading prayer,
From the heart's heart yet again—
That *Columbia*, no more bear
On her brow the seal of Cain!

Hear us, O God of the slave!
Hear us Great Father of Men!
Be *Thy* hand outstretched to save,
Be *Thy* voice heard yet again!

Speak to their souls, who oppress—
Speak to their souls, who would spare—
*Here* guide and strengthen and bless—
Conviction, repentance, bring there.

## "Get Off the Track," Hutchinson Family Singers

Ho! the car, Emancipation,
Rides majestic thro' our nation
Bearing on its train, the story
Liberty! a nation's glory.
Roll it along! Roll it along!
Roll it along! thro' the nation
Freedom's car, Emancipation
Roll it along! Roll it along!
Roll it along! thro' the nation
Freedom's car, Emancipation.

First of all the train, and greater,
Speeds the dauntless Liberator
Onward cheered amid hosannas,
And the waving of free banners.
Roll it along! Roll it along!
Roll it along! spread your banners
While the people shout hosannas.

Men of various predilections,
Frightened, run in all directions;
Merchants, editors, physicians,

Lawyers, priests and politicians.
Get out of the way! Get out of the way!
Get out of the way! every station,
Clear the track of 'mancipation.

Let the ministers and churches
Leave behind sectarian lurches;
Jump on board the car of freedom
Ere it be too late to need them.
Sound the alarm! Sound the alarm!
Sound the alarm! pulpit's thunder!
Ere too late, you see your blunder.

Politicians gazed, astounded,
When, at first our bell resounded:
Freight trains are coming, tell these foxes,
With our votes and ballot boxes.
Jump for your lives! Jump for your lives!
Jump for your lives! politicians,
From your dangerous false positions.

Rail roads to emancipation
Cannot rest on Clay foundation
And the tracks of "The Magician"
Are but rail roads to perdition.
Pull up the rails! Pull up the rails!
Pull up the rails! Emancipation
Cannot rest on such foundation.

All true friends of emancipation,
Haste to freedom's rail road station;
Quick into the cars get seated,
All is ready, and completed.
Put on the steam! Put on the steam!
Put on the steam! All are crying,
And the liberty flags are flying.

Now, again the bell is tolling,
Soon you'll see the car wheels rolling;
Hinder not their destination,
Chartered for emancipation.
Wood up the fire! Wood up the fire!
Wood up the fire! keep it flashing,
While the train goes onward dashing.

Hear the mighty car wheels humming!
Now look out! the engine's coming!
Church and statesmen! hear the thunder!
Clear the track! or you'll fall under.
Get off the track! Get off the track!
Get off the track! all are singing,
While the liberty bell is ringing.

On triumphant, see them bearing,
Through sectarian rubbish tearing;
Th' bell and whistle and the steaming,
Startles thousands from their dreaming.
Look out for the cars! Look out for the cars!
Look out for the cars! while the bell rings,
Ere the sound your funeral knell rings.

See the people run to meet us;
At the depots thousands greet us;
All take seats with exultation,
In the car, Emancipation.
Huzza! Huzza! Huzza! Huzza!
Huzza! Huzza! Emancipation
Soon will bless our happy nation.
Huzza! Huzza!! Huzza!!!

## "The Universalist Sunday School Pic Nic"

*Where shall our Festival be held?*
*Mammon our forest fane has felled!*
*His iron hand has bared the soil—*
*God's temple his unholy spoil.*
*Those solemn aisles, that oft have rung*
*With praise and prayer from hallowed tongue,*
*Where childhood's glancing form and eye*
*Have moved and sparkled joyously,*
*Where sober age, has felt again,*
*Youth's current, course the sluggish vein,*
*Where silent meditation, too,*
*Has caught of Heaven the longed-for view—*
*That sacred summer eve retreat,*
*Where friend met friend in converse sweet—*
*That fairy hall, where erst was spread*
*The rarest treasures, changed to bread,*
*To meet the struggling soul's demand,*
*By the great social magic wand—*

*That place of justice, where the word*
*Was uttered, that deep hearts has stirred,*
*When pressing thousands gathered round,*
*To catch of Freedom's' voice the sound,*
*Freedom from chains of sin and sense,*
*And tyrrany's omnipotence—*
*All these, and more; the shrine where God*
*Has met the suppliant on the sod—*
*All these, and this, are falling now,*
*Where those young oaks their foreheads bow,*
*At mammon's pitiful decree,*
*To the low earth they scorned to see.*
*Where were ye, Nymphs of tree and dell,*
*When on your home destruction fell?*
*When the reverberating stroke*
*First on your startled senses broke?*
*Where are ye now—what grotto lone,*
*Echoes your plaintive exile moan?—*
*Was there no voice to cry forbear!*
*Was there no hand outstretched to spare?*
*No potent power from memory's urn,*
*Backward the murderous edge to turn?*
*Too deep we feel the saddening truth,*
*Nor age mature, nor virtuous youth,*
*Are ever safe from that fell power,*
*That rules the ruin of each hour;*
*Despoils each spirit, as each plain,*
*For its poor estimate of gain!*
*Over the Past's receding track,*
*Inquiringly, as we glance back,*
*The same sad foot-prints mark the scene;*
*On every hand the blight has been;*
*Of old, 'neath Oriental skies,*
*God's house was made, by man, a place of merchandise,*
*But while I mourn, and mourn in vain,*
*That plaintive voice is heard again—*
*"Where shall our festival be held?"*
*"Despair not—though we are expelled*
*"From this so loved, so fair retreat,*
*"God's world is wide, we yet may meet.*
*"Turn thou that tear-dimmed, mourning eye,*
*"Where yon green hill, towers to the sky,*
*"That lovingly above is bent—*
*"There, as of Old, we'll "pitch our tent."*
*"A holy hill, though bald and bare;*
*"The Father still can meet us there;*

"His elder children's record, tell,
"He in "high places" once did dwell—
"His Best-Beloved, too, has said
"His influence everywhere is shed.
"If true the praise, and true the prayer,
"We know our Father will be there."
Then to the Mount of Worship, they
Ascended, on their joyous way—
Childhood, and youth, and age, went by,
With their young pastor, lovingly—
That one, so early called, to break
The bread of life, for Jesus' sake;
Ere scarce the years of man are told,
The shepherd of a hungry fold.
O, God be with him, in his toil;
His dew and sunshine bless the soil!
With all the earnest zeal of youth,
O may he seek and serve the truth—
Ne'er resting in one little part,
To all its influence, bare his heart;
Wisely discreet, yet bravely free,
Teach sinning souls what they should be;
From earth and sense, draw them above,
By influence of law and love;
Like youthful Samuel, lend his ear
The Father's whispered words to hear;
Trusting the future to His power,
Toil, earnest, in the present hour—
Yes, God be with him to the end;
A trusted and a trusting Friend!—
Tent-shielded from the sun's broad light
The day passed, on that holy height;
Sweet converse and kind words were there,
And songs of praise, and earnest prayer,
And when the sun's departing ray
Smiled benediction on the day,
With gladdened spirits they retraced
Their steps, to the accustomed place
Of worship, one more hour to spend
In services that heavenward tend.
And though no spot can ever be
To them what was Tranquillity
Long shall they cherish fondly still,
The Pic Nic upon Baker's Hill.
August, 1844.

## Announcement of August 1, 1844 Celebration in Concord

Announcement of August 1, 1844 celebration in Concord on the anniversary of emancipation in the British West Indies (transcribed from *The Liberator*, July 12, 1844):

To the Friends of Freedom in Middlesex and the neighboring Counties.

All who feel interested in the slave's welfare and the progress of human rights, of whatever sect or sex, age or character, are invited to meet at Concord, on the approaching 1st of August, to celebrate the anniversary of the emancipation of 800,000 slaves in the British West Indies—an event the most note-worthy of modern times, one which appeals to the noblest feelings of the heart; which was stained with no blood, and achieved by no physical strife, but accomplished by the wonder-working power of truth and even-handed justice; which has caused no tears to flow but those of joy, unless the tyrant weeps over victims snatched away; which has proved that obedience to the laws of God is for man's best interest; which has raised thousands from the position of brutes to that of men, and carried the light of knowledge and Christianity to the homes of thousands in the darkness before; and which is, in fact, the crowning glory of Christianity in this age.

The exercises will commence at 11 o'clock, and will consist of singing by an anti-slavery choir, and an address by RALPH WALDO EMERSON. At noon, there will be a collation in the woods—tickets 25 cents—and afterwards, addresses by John Pierpont, S.J. May, F. Douglass, Walter Channing, and other distinguished friends of liberty, whose names will be announced in the next Liberator, as well as the place where the meeting is to be held, in Concord.

It is desirable that the friends who propose coming, should send an estimate of the number that will probably attend from their respective towns, that suitable provision may be made. Please address WM. A. WHITE, Watertown, or Mrs. M.M. BROOKS, Concord.

## Ralph Waldo Emerson Address, August 1, 1844, Concord

AN ADDRESS DELIVERED IN THE COURT-HOUSE IN CONCORD, MASSACHUSETTS, ON 1st AUGUST, 1844, ON THE ANNIVERSARY OF THE EMANCIPATION OF THE NEGROES IN THE BRITISH WEST INDIES.
BY Ralph Waldo Emerson

FRIENDS AND FELLOW CITIZENS,
We are met to exchange congratulations on the anniversary of an event singular in the history of civilization; a day of reason; of the clear light; of that which makes us better than a flock of birds and beasts: a day, which gave the immense fortification of a fact,— of gross history,—to ethical abstractions. It was the settlement, as far as a great Empire was concerned, of a question on which almost every leading citizen in it had taken care to record his vote; one which for many years absorbed the attention of the best

and most eminent of mankind. I might well hesitate, from other studies, and without the smallest claim to be a special laborer in this work of humanity, to undertake to set this matter before you; which ought rather to be done by a strict cooperation of many well- advised persons; but I shall not apologize for my weakness. In this cause, no man's weakness is any prejudice; it has a thousand sons; if one man cannot speak, ten others can; and whether by the wisdom of its friends, or by the folly of the adversaries; by speech and by silence; by doing and by omitting to do, it goes forward. Therefore I will speak, or,—not I, but the might of liberty in my weakness. The subject is said to have the property of making dull men eloquent.

It has been in all men's experience a marked effect of the enterprise in behalf of the African, to generate an over-bearing and defying spirit. The institution of slavery seems to its opponent to have but one side, and he feels that none but a stupid or a malignant person can hesitate on a view of the facts. Under such an impulse, I was about to say, If any cannot speak, or cannot hear the words of freedom, let him go hence,—I had almost said, Creep into your grave, the universe has no need of you! But I have thought better: let him not go. When we consider what remains to be done for this interest, in this country, the dictates of humanity make us tender of such as are not yet persuaded. The hardest selfishness is to be borne with. Let us withhold every reproachful, and, if we can, every indignant remark. In this cause, we must renounce our temper, and the risings of pride. If there be any man who thinks the ruin of a race of men a small matter, compared with the last decoration and completions of his own comfort,—who would not so much as part with his ice-cream, to save them from rapine and manacles, I think, I must not hesitate to satisfy that man, that also his cream and vanilla are safer and cheaper, by placing the negro nation on a fair footing, than by robbing them. If the Virginian piques himself on the picturesque luxury of his vassalage, on the heavy Ethiopian manners of his house-servants, their silent obedience, their hue of bronze, their turbaned heads, and would not exchange them for the more intelligent but precarious hired-service of whites, I shall not refuse to show him, that when their free-papers are made out, it will still be their interest to remain on his estate, and that the oldest planters of Jamaica are convinced, that it is cheaper to pay wages, than to own the slave.

The history of mankind interests us only as it exhibits a steady gain of truth and right, in the incessant conflict which it records, between the material and the moral nature. From the earliest monuments, it appears, that one race was victim, and served the other races. In the oldest temples of Egypt, negro captives are painted on the tombs of kings, in such attitudes as to show that they are on the point of being executed; and Herodotus, our oldest historian, relates that the Troglodytes hunted the Ethiopians in four-horse-chariots. From the earliest time, the negro has been an article of luxury to the commercial nations. So has it been, down to the day that has just dawned on the world. Language must be raked, the secrets of slaughter-houses and infamous holes that cannot front the day, must be ransacked, to tell what negro-slavery has been. These men, our benefactors, as they are producers of corn and wine, of coffee, of tobacco, of cotton, of sugar, of rum, and brandy, gentle and joyous themselves, and producers of comfort and luxury for the civilized world,—there seated in the finest climates of the globe, children of the sun,—I am heart-sick when I read how they came there, and how they are kept there. Their case was left out of the mind and out of the heart of their brothers. The prizes of society, the trumpet of fame, the privileges of learning, of culture, of religion, the decencies and joys of marriage, honor, obedience, personal authority, and a perpetual melioration into a finer civility, these were for all, but not for them. For the negro, was the slave-ship to begin with, in whose filthy hold he sat in irons, unable to lie down; bad food, and insufficiency of that; disfranchisement; no property in the rags that covered him; no marriage, no right in the poor black woman that cherished him in her bosom,—no right to the children of his body; no security from the humors, none from the crimes, none from the appetites of his master: toil, famine, insult, and flogging; and, when he sunk in the furrow, no wind of good fame blew over him, no priest of salvation visited him with glad tidings: but he went down to death, with dusky dreams of African shadow-catchers and Obeahs hunting him. Very sad was the negro tradition, that the Great Spirit, in the beginning, offered the black man, whom he loved better than the buckra or white, his choice of two boxes, a big and a little one. The black man was greedy, and chose the largest. "The buckra box was full up with pen, paper, and whip, and the negro box with hoe and bill; and hoe and bill for negro to this day."

But the crude element of good in human affairs must work and ripen, spite of whips, and plantation-laws, and West Indian interest. Conscience rolled on its pillow, and could not sleep. We sympathize very tenderly here with the poor aggrieved planter, of whom so many unpleasant things are said; but if we saw the whip applied to old men, to tender women; and, undeniably, though I shrink to say so,—pregnant women set in the treadmill for refusing to work, when, not they, but the eternal law of animal nature refused to work;—if we saw men's backs flayed with cowhides, and "hot rum poured on, superinduced with brine or pickle, rubbed in with a cornhusk, in the scorching heat of the sun;"—if we saw the runaways hunted with blood-hounds into swamps and hills; and, in cases of passion, a planter throwing his negro into a copper of boiling cane-juice,—if we saw these things with eyes, we too should wince. They are not pleasant sights. The blood is moral: the blood is anti-slavery: it runs cold in the veins: the stomach rises with disgust, and curses slavery. Well, so it happened; a good man or woman, a country- boy or girl, it would so fall out, once in a while saw these injuries, and had the indiscretion to tell of them. The horrid story ran and flew; the winds blew it all over the world. They who heard it, asked their rich and great friends, if it was true, or only missionary lies. The richest and greatest, the prime minister of England, the kings privy council were obliged to say, that it was too true. It became plain to all men, the more this business was looked into, that the crimes and cruelties of the slave-traders and slave-owners could not be overstated. The more it was searched, the more shocking anecdotes came up,—things not to be spoken. Humane persons who were informed of the reports, insisted on proving them. Granville Sharpe was accidentally made acquainted with the sufferings of a slave, whom a West Indian planter had brought with him to London, and had beaten with a pistol on his head so badly, that his whole body became diseased, and the man useless to his master, who left him to go whither he pleased. The man applied to Mr. William Sharpe, a charitable surgeon, who attended the diseases of the poor. In process of time, he was healed. Granville Sharpe found him at his brother's, and procured a place for him in an apothecary's shop. The master accidentally met his recovered slave, and instantly endeavored to get possession of him again. Sharpe protected the slave. In consulting with the lawyers, they told

Sharpe the laws were against him. Sharpe would not believe it; no prescription on earth could ever render such iniquities legal. But the decisions are against you, and Lord Mansfield, now chief justice of England, leans to the decisions. Sharpe instantly sat down and gave himself to the study of English law for more than two years, until he had proved that the opinions relied on of Talbot and Yorke, were incompatible with the former English decisions, and with the whole spirit of English law. He published his book in 1769; and he so filled the heads and hearts of his advocates, that when he brought the case of George Somerset, another slave, before Lord Mansfield, the slavish decisions were set aside, and equity affirmed. There is a sparkle of God's righteousness in Lord Mansfield's judgment, which does the heart good. Very unwilling had that great lawyer been to reverse the late decisions; he suggested twice from the bench, in the course of the trial, how the question might be got rid of: but the hint was not taken; the case was adjourned again and again, and judgment delayed. At last judgment was demanded, and on the 22d June, 1772, Lord Mansfield is reported to have decided in these words; "Immemorial usage preserves the memory of positive law, long after all traces of the occasion, reason, authority, and time of its introduction, are lost; and in a case so odious as the condition of slaves, must be taken strictly (tracing the subject to natural principles, the claim of slavery never can be supported.) The power claimed by this return never was in use here. We cannot say the cause set forth by this return is allowed or approved of by the laws of this kingdom; and therefore the man must be discharged."

This decision established the principle that the air of England is too pure for any slave to breathe, but the wrongs in the islands were not thereby touched. Public attention, however, was drawn that way, and the methods of the stealing and the transportation from Africa, became noised abroad. The Quakers got the story. In their plain meeting-ho uses; and prim dwellings, this dismal agitation got entrance. They were rich: they owned for debt, or by inheritance, island property; they were religious, tender-hearted men and women; and they had to hear the news, and digest it as they could. Six Quakers met in London on the 6th July, 1783; William Dillwyn, Samuel Hoar, George Harrison, Thomas Knowles, John Lloyd, Joseph Woods, "to consider what step they should take for the relief and liberation of the negro slaves in the West Indies," and for the discouragement of the slave-trade on the coast of Africa. They made friends and raised money for the slave; they interested their Yearly Meeting; and all English and all American Quakers. John Woolman of New Jersey, whilst yet an apprentice, was uneasy in his mind when he was set to write a bill of sale of a negro, for his master. He gave his testimony against the traffic, in Maryland and Virginia. Thomas Clarkson was a youth at Cambridge, England, when the subject given out for a Latin prize dissertation, was, "Is it right to make slaves of others against their will?" He wrote an essay, and won the prize; but he wrote too well for his own peace; he began to ask himself, if these things could be true; and if they were, he could no longer rest. He left Cambridge; he fell in with the six Quakers. They engaged him to act for them. He himself interested Mr. Wilberforce in the matter. The shipmasters in that trade were the greatest miscreants, and guilty of every barbarity to their own crews. Clarkson went to Bristol, made himself acquainted with the interior of the slave-ships, and the details of the trade. The facts confirmed his sentiment, "that Providence had never made that to be wise, which was immoral, and that the slave-trade was as impolitic as it was unjust;" that it was found peculiarly fatal to those employed in it. More seamen died in that trade, in one year, than in the whole remaining trade of the country in two. Mr. Pitt and Mr. Fox were drawn into the generous enterprise. In 1788, the House of Commons voted Parliamentary inquiry. In 1791, a bill to abolish the trade was brought in by Wilberforce, and supported by him, and by Fox, and Burke, and Pitt, with the utmost ability and faithfulness; resisted by the planters, and the whole West Indian interest, and lost. During the next sixteen years, ten times, year after year, the attempt was renewed by Mr. Wilberforce, and ten times defeated by the planters. The king, and all the royal family but one, were against it. These debates are instructive, as they show on what grounds the trade was assailed and defended. Every thing generous, wise, and sprightly is sure to come to the attack. On the other part, are found cold prudence, barefaced selfishness, and silent votes. But the nation was aroused to enthusiasm. Every horrid fact became known. In 1791, three hundred thousand persons in Britain pledged themselves to abstain from all articles of island produce. The planters were obliged to give way; and in 1807, on the 25th March, the bill passed, and the slave-trade was abolished.

The assailants of slavery had early agreed to limit their political action on this subject to the abolition of the trade, but Granville Sharpe, as a matter of conscience, whilst he acted as chairman of the London Committee, felt constrained to record his protest against the limitation, declaring that slavery was as much a crime against the Divine law, as the slave-trade. The trade, under false flags, went on as before. In 1821, according to official documents presented to the American government by the Colonization Society, 200,000 slaves were deported from Africa. Nearly 30,000 were landed in the port of Havana alone. In consequence of the dangers of the trade growing out of the act of abolition, ships were built sharp for swiftness, and with a frightful disregard of the comfort of the victims they were destined to transport. They carried five, six, even seven hundred stowed in a ship built so narrow as to be unsafe, being made just broad enough on the beam to keep the sea. In attempting to make its escape from the pursuit of a man-of-war, one ship flung five hundred slaves alive into the sea. These facts went into Parliament. In the islands, was an ominous state of cruel and licentious society; every house had a dungeon attached to it; every slave was worked by the whip. There is no end to the tragic anecdotes in the municipal records of the colonies. The boy was set to strip and to flog his own mother to blood, for a small offence. Looking in the face of his master by the negro was held to be violence by the island courts. He was worked sixteen hours, and his ration by law, in some islands, was a pint of flour and one salt herring a day. He suffered insult, stripes, mutilation, at the humor of the master: iron collars were riveted on their necks with iron prongs ten inches long; capsicum pepper was rubbed in. the eyes of the females; and they were done to death with the most shocking levity between the master and manager, without fine or inquiry. And when, at last, some Quakers, Moravians, and Wesleyan and Baptist missionaries, following in the steps of Carey and Ward in the East Indies, had been moved to come and cheer the poor victim with the hope of some reparation, in a future world, of the wrongs he suffered in this, these missionaries were persecuted by the planters, their lives threatened, their chapels burned, and the negroes furiously forbidden to go near them. These outrages rekindled the flame of British indignation. Petitions poured into Parliament: a million persons signed their names to these; and in 1833, on the 14th May, Lord Stanley, minister of the colonies, introduced into the House of Commons his bill for the Emancipation.

The scheme of the minister, with such modification as it received in the legislature, proposed gradual emancipation; that on 1st August, 1834, all persons now slaves should be entitled to be registered as apprenticed laborers, and to acquire thereby all the rights and privileges of freemen, subject to the restriction of laboring under certain conditions. These conditions were, that the prædials should owe three fourths of the profits of their labor to their masters for six years, and the non-prædials for four years. The other fourth of the apprentice's time was to be his own, which he might sell to his master, or to other persons; and at the end of the term of years fixed, he should be free. With these provisions and conditions, the bill proceeds, in the twelfth section, in the following terms. "Be it enacted, that all and every person who, on the 1st August, 1834, shall be holden in slavery within any such British colony as aforesaid, shall upon and from and after the said 1st August, become and be to all intents and purposes free, and discharged of and from all manner of slavery, and shall be absolutely and forever manumitted; and that the children thereafter born to any such persons, and the offspring of such children, shall, in like manner, be free from their birth; and that from and after the 1st August, 1834, slavery shall be and is hereby utterly and forever abolished and declared unlawful throughout the British colonies, plantations, and possessions abroad."

The ministers, having estimated the slave products of the colonies in annual exports of sugar, rum, and coffee, at 1,500,000 per annum, estimated the total value of the slave-property at 30,000,000 pounds sterling, and proposed to give the planters, as a compensation for so much of the slaves' time as the act took from them, 20,000,000 pounds sterling, to be divided into nineteen shares for the nineteen colonies, and to be distributed to the owners of slaves by commissioners, whose appointment and duties were regulated by the Act. After much debate, the bill passed by large majorities.

The apprenticeship system is understood to have proceeded from Lord Brougham, and was by him urged on his colleagues, who, it is said, were inclined to the policy of immediate emancipation. The colonial legislatures received the act of Parliament with various degrees of displeasure, and, of course, every provision of the bill was criticised with severity. The new relation between the master and the apprentice, it was feared, would be mischievous; for the bill required the appointment of magistrates, who should hear every complaint of the apprentice, and see that justice was done him. It was feared that the interest of the master and servant would now produce perpetual discord between them. In the island of Antigua, containing 37,000 people, 30,000 being negroes, these objections had such weight, that the legislature rejected the apprenticeship system, and adopted absolute emancipation. In the other islands the system of the ministry was accepted.

The reception of it by the negro population was equal in nobleness to the deed. The negroes were called together by the missionaries and by the planters, and the news explained to them. On the night of the 31st July, they met everywhere at their churches and chapels, and at midnight, when the clock struck twelve, on their knees, the silent, weeping assembly became men; they rose and embraced each other ; they cried, they sung, they prayed, they were wild with joy, but there was no riot, no feasting. I have never read anything in history more touching than the moderation of the negroes. Some

American captains left the shore and put to sea, anticipating insurrection and general murder. With far different thoughts, the negroes spent the hour in their huts and chapels. I will not repeat to you the well-known paragraph, in which Messrs. Thome and Kimball, the commissioners sent out in the year 1837 by the American Anti-slavery Society, describe the occurrences of that night in the island of Antigua. It has been quoted in every newspaper, and Dr. Channing has given it additional fame. But I must be indulged in quoting a few sentences from the pages that follow it, narrating the behavior of the emancipated people on the next day.

"The first of August came on Friday, and a release was proclaimed from all work until the next Monday. The day was chiefly spent by the great mass of the negroes in the churches and chapels. The clergy and missionaries throughout the island were actively engaged, seizing the opportunity to enlighten the people on all the duties and responsibilities of their new relation, and urging them to the attainment of that higher liberty with which Christ maketh his children free. In every quarter, we were assured, the day was like a sabbath. Work had ceased. The hum of business was still: tranquility pervaded the towns and country. The planters informed us, that they went to the chapels where their own people were assembled, greeted them, shook hands with them, and exchanged the most hearty good wishes. At Grace Hill, there were at least a thousand persons around the Moravian Chapel who could not get in. For once the house of God suffered violence, and the violent took it by force. At Grace Bay, the people, all dressed in white, formed a procession, and walked arm in arm into the chapel. We were told that the dress of the negroes on that occasion was uncommonly simple and modest. There was not the least disposition to gaiety. Throughout the island, there was not a single dance known of, either day or night, nor so much as a fiddle played.

On the next Monday morning, with very few exceptions, every negro on every plantation was in the field at his work. In some places, they waited to see their master, to know what bargain he would make; but, for the most part, throughout the islands, nothing painful occurred. In June, 1835, the ministers, Lord Aberdeen and Sir George Grey, declared to the Parliament, that the system worked well; that now for ten months, from 1st August, 1834, no injury or violence had been offered to any white, and only one black had been hurt in 800,000 negroes: and, contrary to many sinister predictions, that the new crop of island produce would not fall short of that of the last year.

But the habit of oppression was not destroyed by a law and a day of jubilee. It soon appeared in all the islands, that the planters were disposed to use their old privileges, and overwork the apprentices; to take from them, under various pretences, their fourth part of their time; and to exert the same licentious despotism as before. The negroes complained to the magistrates, and to the governor. In the island of Jamaica, this ill blood continually grew worse. The governors, Lord Belmore, the Earl of Sligo, and afterwards Sir Lionel Smith, (a governor of their own class, who had been sent out to gratify the planters,) threw themselves on the side of the oppressed, and are at constant quarrel with the angry and bilious island legislature. Nothing can exceed the ill humor and sulkiness of the addresses of this assembly.

I may here express a general remark, which the history of slavery seems to justify, that it is not founded solely on the avarice of the planter. We sometimes say, the planter does not want slaves, he only wants the immunities and the luxuries which the slaves yield him; give him money, give him a machine that will yield him as much money as the slaves, and he will thankfully let them go. He has no love of slavery, he wants luxury, and he will pay even this price of crime and danger for it. But I think experience does not warrant this favorable distinction, but shows the existence, beside the covetousness, of a bitterer element, the love of power, the voluptuousness of holding a human being in his absolute control. We sometimes observe, that spoiled children contract a habit of annoying quite wantonly those who have charge of them, and seem to measure their own sense of well-being, not by what they do, but by the degree of reaction they can cause. It is vain to get rid of them by not minding them: if purring and humming is, not noticed, they squeal and screech; then if you chide and console them, they find the experiment succeeds, and they begin again. The child will sit in your arms contented, provided you do nothing. If you take a book and read, he commences hostile operations. The planter is the spoiled child of his unnatural habits, and has contracted in his indolent and luxurious climate the need of excitement by irritating and tormenting his slave.

Sir Lionel Smith defended the poor negro girls, prey to the licentiousness of the planters; they shall not be whipped with tamarind rods, if they do not comply with their masters will; he defended the negro women; they should not be made to dig the cane-holes, (which is the very hardest of the field-work;) he defended the Baptist preachers and the stipendiary magistrates, who are the negroes' friends, from the power of the planter. The power of the planters, however, to oppress, was greater than the power of the apprentice and of his guardians to withstand. Lord Brougham and Mr. Buxton declared that the planter had not fulfilled his part in the contract, whilst the apprentices had fulfilled theirs; and demanded that the emancipation should be hastened, and the apprenticeship abolished. Parliament was compelled to pass additional laws for the defence and security of the negro, and in ill humor at these acts, the great island of Jamaica, with a population of half a million, and 300,000 negroes, early in 1838, resolved to throw up the two remaining years of apprenticeship, and to emancipate absolutely on the 1st August, 1838 in British Guiana, in Dominica, the same resolution had been earlier taken with more good will; and the other islands fell into the measure; so that on the 1st August, 1838, the shackles dropped from every British slave. The accounts which we have from all parties, both from the planters, and those too who were originally most opposed to the measure, and from the new freemen, are of the most satisfactory kind. The manner in which the new festival was celebrated, brings tears to the eyes. The First of August, 1838, was observed in Jamaica as a day of thanksgiving and prayer. Sir Lionel Smith, the governor, writes to the British Ministry, It is impossible for me to do justice to the good order, decorum, and gratitude, which the whole laboring population manifested on that happy occasion. Though joy beamed on every countenance, it was throughout tempered with solemn thankfulness to God, and the churches and chapels were everywhere filled with these happy people in humble offering of praise."

The Queen, in her speech to the Lords and Commons, praised the conduct of the emancipated population: and, in 1840, Sir Charles Metcalfe, the new governor of Jamaica, in his address to the Assembly, expressed himself to that late exasperated body in these terms. "All those who are acquainted with the state of the island, know that our emancipated population are as free, as independent in their conduct, as well-conditioned, as much in the enjoyment of abundance, and as strongly sensible of the blessings of liberty, as any that we know of in any country. All disqualifications and distinctions of color have ceased; men of all colors have equal rights in law, and an equal footing in society, and every man's position is settled by the same circumstances which regulate that point in other free countries, where no difference of color exists. It may be asserted, without fear of denial, that the former slaves of Jamaica are now as secure in all social rights, as freeborn Britons." He further describes the erection of numerous churches, chapels, and schools, which the new population required, and adds that more are still demanded. The legislature, in their reply, echo the governor's statement, and say, "The peaceful demeanor of the emancipated population redounds to their own credit, and affords a proof of their continued comfort and prosperity."

I said, this event is signal in the history of civilization. There are many styles of civilization, and not one only. Ours is full of barbarities. There are many faculties in n-ian, each of which takes its turn of activity, and that faculty which is paramount in any period, and exerts itself through the strongest nation, determines the civility of that age; and each age thinks its own the perfection of reason. Our culture is very cheap and intelligible. Unroof any house, and you shall find it. The well-being consists in having a sufficiency of coffee and toast, with a daily newspaper; a well-glazed parlor, with marbles, mirrors, and centre-table; and the excitement of a few parties and a few rides in a year. Such as one house, such are all. The owner of a New York manor imitates the mansion and equipage of the London nobleman; the Boston merchant rivals his brother of New York; and the villages copy Boston. There have been nations elevated by great sentiments. Such was the civility of Sparta and the Dorian race, whilst it was defective in some of the chief elements of ours. That of Athens, again, lay in an intellect dedicated to beauty. That of Asia Minor in poetry, music, and arts; that of Palestine in piety; that of Rome in military arts and virtues, exalted by a prodigious magnanimity; that of China and Japan in the last exaggeration of decorum and etiquette. Our civility, England determines the style of, inasmuch as England is the strongest of the family of existing nations, and as we are the expansion of that people. It is that of a trading nation; it is a shop-keeping civility. The English lord is a retired shopkeeper, and has the prejudices and timidities of that profession. And we are shopkeepers, and have acquired the vices and virtues that belong to trade. We peddle, we truck, we sail, we row, we ride in cars, we creep in teams, we go in canals,—to market, and for the sale of goods. The national aim and employment streams into our ways of thinking, our laws, our habits, and our manners. The customer is the immediate jewel of our souls. Him we flatter, him we feast, compliment, vote for, and will not contradict. It was or it seemed the dictate of trade, to keep the negro down. We had found a race who were less warlike, and less energetic shopkeepers than we; who had very little skill in trade. We found it very convenient to keep them at work, since, by the aid of a little whipping, we could get their work for nothing but their board and the cost of whips. What if it cost a few unpleasant scenes on the coast of Africa? That was a great way off; and the scenes could be endured by some sturdy, unscrupulous fellows, who could go for high wages and bring us the men, and need not trouble our ears with the disagreeable particulars. If any mention was made of homicide, madness, adultery, and intolerable tortures, we would let the church-bells ring louder, the church-organ swell its peal, and drown the hideous sound. The sugar they raised was excellent: nobody tasted blood in it. The coffee was fragrant; the tobacco was incense; the brandy made nations happy the cotton clothed the world. What! all raised by these men, and no wages? Excellent! What a convenience! They seemed created by providence to bear the heat and the whipping, and make these fine articles.

But unhappily, most unhappily, gentlemen, man is born with intellect, as well as with a love of sugar, and with a sense of justice, as well as a taste for strong drink. These ripened, as well as those. You could not educate him, you could not get any poetry, any wisdom, any beauty in woman, any strong and commanding character in man, but these absurdities would still come flashing out, these absurdities of a demand for justice, a generosity for the weak and oppressed. Unhappily too, for the planter, the laws of nature are in harmony with each other: that which the head and the heart demand, is found to be, in the long run, for what the grossest calculator calls his advantage. The moral sense is always supported by the permanent interest of the parties. Else, I know not how, in our world, any good would ever get done. It was shown to the planters that they, as well as the negroes, were slaves; that though they paid no wages, they got very poor work; that their estates were ruining them, under the finest climate; and that they needed the severest monopoly laws at home to keep them from bankruptcy. The oppression of the slave recoiled on them. They were full of vices; their children were lumps of pride, sloth, sensuality and rottenness. The position of woman was nearly as bad as it could be, and, like other robbers, they could not sleep in security. Many planters have said, since the emancipation, that, before that day, they were the greatest slaves on the estates. Slavery is no scholar, no improver; it does not love the whistle of the railroad; it does not love the newspaper, the mailbag, a college, a book, or a preacher who has the absurd whim of saying what he thinks; it does not increase the white population; it does not improve the soil; everything goes to decay. For these reasons, the islands proved bad customers to England. It was very easy for manufacturers less shrewd than those of Birmingham and Manchester to see, that if the state of things in the islands was altered, if the slaves had wages, the slaves would be clothed, would build houses, would fill them with tools, with pottery, with crockery, with hardware; and negro women love fine clothes as well as white women. In every naked negro of those thousands, they saw a future customer. Meantime, they saw further, that the slave-trade, by keeping in barbarism the whole coast of eastern Africa, deprives them of countries and nations of customers, if once freedom and civility, and European manners could get a foothold there. But the trade could not be abolished, whilst this hungry West Indian market, with an appetite like the grave, cried, More, more, bring me a hundred a day; they could not expect any mitigation in the madness of the poor African war-chiefs. These considerations opened the eyes of the dullest in Britain. More than this, the West Indian estate was owned or mortgaged in England, and the owner and the mortgagee had very plain intimations that the feeling of English liberty was gaining every hour new mass and velocity, and the hostility to such as resisted it, would be fatal. The House of Commons would destroy the protection of island produce, and interfere on English politics in the island legislation: so they hastened to make the best of their position, and accepted the bill.

These considerations, I doubt not, had their weight, the interest of trade, the interest of the revenue, and, moreover, the good fame of the action. It was inevitable that men should feel these motives. But they do not appear to have had an excessive or unreasonable weight. On reviewing this history, I think the whole transaction reflects infinite honor on the people and parliament of England. It was a stately spectacle, to see the cause of human rights argued with so much patience and generosity, and with such a mass of evidence before that powerful people. It is a creditable incident in the history, that when, in 1789, the first privy-council report of evidence on the trade, a bulky folio, (embodying all the facts which the London Committee had been engaged for years in collecting, and all the examinations before the council,) was presented to the House of Commons, a late day being named for the discussion, in order to give members time,—Mr. Wilberforce, Mr. Pitt, the prime minister, and other gentlemen, took advantage of the postponement, to retire into the country, to read the report. For months and years the bill was debated, with some consciousness of the extent of its relations by the first citizens of England, the foremost men of the earth; every argument was weighed, every particle of evidence was sifted, and laid in the scale; and, at last, the right triumphed, the poor man was vindicated, and the oppressor was flung out. I know that England has the advantage of trying the question at a wide distance from the spot where the nuisance exists the planters are not, excepting in rare examples, members of the legislature. The extent of the empire, and the magnitude and number of other questions crowding into court, keep this one in balance, and prevent it from obtaining that ascendency, and being urged with that intemperance, which a question of property tends to acquire. There are causes in the composition of the British legislature, and the relation of its leaders to the country and to Europe, which exclude much that is pitiful and injurious in other legislative assemblies. From these reasons, the question was discussed with a rare independence and magnanimity. It was not narrowed down to a paltry electioneering trap, and, I must say, a delight in justice, an honest tenderness for the poor negro, for man suffering these wrongs, combined with the national pride, which refused to give the support of English soil, or the protection of the English flag, to these disgusting violations of nature.

Forgive me, fellow citizens, if I own to you, that in the last few days that my attention has been occupied with this history, I have not been able to read a page of it, without the most painful comparisons. Whilst I have read of England, I have thought of New England. Whilst I have meditated in my solitary walks on the magnanimity of the English Bench and Senate, reaching out the benefit of the law to the most helpless citizen in her world-wide realm, I have found myself oppressed by other thoughts. As I have walked in the pastures and along the edge of woods, I could not keep my imagination on those agreeable figures, for other images that intruded on me. I could not see the great vision of the patriots and senators who have adopted the slaves cause:—they turned their backs on me. No: I see other pictures—of mean men: I see very poor, very ill-clothed, very ignorant men, not surrounded by happy friends,—to be plain,—poor black men of obscure employment as mariners, cooks, or stewards, in ships, yet citizens of this our Commonwealth of Massachusetts,—freeborn as we,— whom the slave-laws of the States of South Carolina, Georgia, and Louisiana, have arrested in the vessels in which they visited those ports, and shut up in jails so long as the vessel remained in port, with the stringent addition, that if the shipmaster fails to pay the costs of this official arrest, and the board in jail, these citizens are to be sold for slaves, to pay that expense. This man, these men, I see, and no law to save them. Fellow citizens, this crime will not be hushed up any longer. I have learned that a citizen of Nantucket, walking in New Orleans, found a freeborn citizen of Nantucket, a man, too, of great personal worth, and, as it happened, very dear to him, as having saved his own life, working chained in the streets of that city, kidnapped by such a process as this. In the sleep of the laws, the private interference of two excellent citizens of Boston has, I have ascertained, rescued several natives of this State from these southern prisons. Gentlemen, I thought the deck of a Massachusetts ship was as much the territory of Massachusetts, as the floor on which we stand. It should be as sacred as the temple of God. The poorest fishing-smack, that floats under the shadow of an iceberg in the northern seas, or hunts the whale in the southern ocean, should be encompassed by her laws with comfort and protection, as much as within the arms of Cape Ann and Cape Cod. And this kidnapping is suffered within our own land and federation, whilst the fourth article of the Constitution of the United States ordains in terms, that, "The citizens of each State shall be entitled to all privileges and immunities of citizens in the several States." If such a damnable outrage can be committed on the person of a citizen with impunity, let the Governor break the broad seal of the State; he bears the sword in vain. The Governor of Massachusetts is a trifler: the State-house in Boston is a play-house: the General Court is a dishonored body: if they make laws which they cannot execute. The great-hearted Puritans have left no posterity. The rich men may walk in State-street, but they walk without honor; and the farmers may brag their democracy in the country, but they are disgraced men. If the State has no power to defend its own people in its own shipping, because it has delegated that power to the Federal Government, has it no representation in the Federal Government? Are those men dumb? I am no lawyer, and cannot indicate the forms applicable to the case, but here is something which transcends all forms. Let the senators and representatives of the State, containing a population of a million freemen, go in a body before the Congress, and say, that they have a demand to make on them so imperative, that all functions of government must stop, until it is satisfied. If ordinary legislation cannot reach it, then extraordinary must be applied. The Congress should instruct the President to send to those ports of Charleston, Savannah, and New Orleans, such orders and such force, as should release, forthwith, all such citizens of Massachusetts as were holden in prison without the allegation of any crime, and should set on foot the strictest inquisition to discover where such persons, brought into slavery by these local laws, at any time heretofore, may now be. That first;—and then, let order be taken to indemnify all such as have been incarcerated. As for dangers to the Union, from such demands!—the Union is already at an end, when the first citizen of Massachusetts is thus outraged. Is it an union and covenant in which the State of Massachusetts agrees to be imprisoned, and the State of Carolina to imprison? Gentlemen, I am loath to say harsh things, and perhaps I know too little of politics for the smallest weight)t to attach to any censure of mine,—but I am at a loss how to characterize the tameness and silence of the two senators and the ten representatives of the State at Washington. To what purpose, have we clothed each of those representatives with the power of seventy thousand persons, and each senator with near half a million, if they are to sit dumb at their desks, and see their constituents captured and sold;—perhaps to gentlemen sitting by them in the hall? There is a scandalous rumor that has been swelling louder of late years, perhaps it is wholly false,—that members are bullied into silence by southern gentlemen. It is so easy to omit to speak, or even to be absent when delicate things are to be handled. I may as well say what all men feel, that whilst our very amiable and very innocent representatives and senators at Washington, are accomplished lawyers and merchants, and very eloquent at dinners and at caucuses, there is a disastrous want of men from New England. I would gladly make exceptions, and you will not suffer me to forget one eloquent old man, in whose veins the blood of Massachusetts rolls, and who singly has defended the freedom of speech, and the rights of the free, against the usurpation of the slave-holder. But the reader of Congressional debates, in New England, is perplexed to see with what admirable sweetness and patience the majority of the free States, are schooled and ridden by the minority of slave-holders. What if we should send thither representatives who were a particle less amiable and less innocent? I entreat you, sirs, let not this stain attach, let not this misery accumulate any longer. If the managers of our political parties are too prudent and too cold;—if, most unhappily, the ambitious class of young men and political men have found out, that these neglected victims and without weight that are poor, that they have no graceful hospitalities to offer; no valuable business to throw into any man's hands, no strong vote to cast at the elections; and therefore may with impunity be left in their chains or to the chance of chains, then let the citizens in their primary capacity take tip their cause on this very ground, and say to the government of the State, and of the Union, that government exists to defend the weak and the poor and the injured party; the rich and the strong can better take care of themselves. And as an omen and assurance of success, I point you to the bright example which England set you, on this day, ten years ago.

There are other comparisons and other imperative duties which come sadly to mind,—but I do not wish to darken the hours of this day by crimination; I turn gladly to the rightful theme, to the bright aspects of the occasion.

This event was a moral revolution. The history of it is before you. Here was no prodigy, no fabulous hero, no Trojan horse, no bloody war, but all was achieved by plain means of plain men, working not under a leader, but under a sentiment. Other revolutions have been the insurrection of the oppressed; this was the repentance of the tyrant. It was the masters revolting from their mastery. The slave-holder said, I will not hold slaves. The end was noble, and the means were pure. Hence, the elevation and pathos of this chapter of history. The lives of the advocates are pages of greatness, and the connexion of the eminent senators with this question, constitutes the immortalizing moments of those men's lives. The bare enunciation of the theses, at which the lawyers and legislators arrived, gives a glow to the heart of the reader. Lord Chancellor Northington is the author of the famous sentence, "As soon as any man puts his foot on English ground, he becomes free." "I was a slave," said the counsel of Somerset, speaking for his client, "for I was in America: I am now in a country, where the common rights of mankind are known and regarded." Granville Sharpe filled the ear of the judges with the sound principles, that had from time to time been affirmed by the legal authorities. "Derived power cannot be superior to the power from which it is derived." "The reasonableness of the law is the soul of the law." "It is better to suffer every evil, than to consent to any." Out it would come, the God's truth, out it came, like a bolt from a cloud, for all the mumbling of the lawyers. One feels very sensibly in all this history that a great heart and soul are behind there, superior to any man, and making use of each, in turn, and infinitely attractive to every person according to the degree of reason in his own mind, so that this cause has had the power to draw to it every particle of talent and of worth in England, from the beginning. All the great geniuses of the British senate, Fox, Pitt, Burke, Grenville, Sheridan, Grey, Canning, ranged themselves on its side; the poet Cowper wrote for it: Franklin, Jefferson, Washington, in this country, all recorded their votes. All men remember the subtlety and the fire of indignation, which the Edinburgh Review contributed to the cause; and every liberal mind, poet, preacher, moralist, statesman, has had the fortune to appear somewhere for this cause. On the other part, appeared the reign of pounds and shillings, and all manner of rage and stupidity; a resistance which drew from Mr. Huddlestone in Parliament the observation, "That a curse attended this trade even in the mode of defending it. By a certain fatality, none but the vilest arguments were brought forward, which corrupted the very persons who used them. Every one of these was built on the narrow ground of interest, of pecuniary profit, of sordid gain, in opposition to every motive that had reference to humanity, justice, and religion, or to that great principle which comprehended them all."—This moral force perpetually reinforces and dignities the friends of this cause. It gave that tenacity to their point which has insured ultimate triumph; and it gave that superiority in reason, in imagery, in eloquence, which makes in all countries anti-slavery meetings so attractive to the people, and has made it a proverb in Massachusetts, that, "eloquence is dog-cheap at the anti-slavery chapel?"

I will say further, that we are indebted mainly to this movement, and to the continuers of it, for the popular discussion of every point of practical ethics, and a reference of every question to the absolute standard. It is notorious, that the political, religious, and social schemes, with which the minds of men are now most occupied, have been matured, or at least broached, in the free and daring discussions of these assemblies. Men have become aware through the emancipation, and kindred events, of the presence of powers, which, in their days of darkness, they had overlooked. Virtuous men will not again rely on political agents. They have found out the deleterious effect of political association. Up to this day, we have allowed to statesmen a paramount social standing, and we bow low to them as to the great. We cannot extend this deference to them any longer. The secret cannot be kept, that the seats of power are filled by underlings, ignorant, timid, and selfish, to a degree to destroy all claim, excepting that on compassion, to the society of the just and generous. What happened notoriously to an American ambassador in England, that he found himself compelled to palter, and to disguise the fact that he was a slave-breeder, happens to men of state. Their vocation is a presumption against them, among well-meaning people. The superstition respecting power and office, is going to the ground. The stream of human affairs flows its own way, and is very little affected by the activity of legislators. What great masses of men wish done, will be done; and they do not wish it for a freak, but because it is their state and natural end. There are now other energies than force, other than political, which no man in future can allow himself to disregard. There is direct conversation and influence. A man is to make himself felt, by his proper force. The tendency of things runs steadily to this point, namely, to put every man on his merits, and to give him so much power as he naturally exerts—no more, no less. Of course, the timid and base persons, all who are conscious of no worth in themselves, and who owe all their place to the opportunities which the old order of things allowed them to deceive and defraud men, shudder at the change, and would fain silence every honest voice, and lock up every house where liberty and innovation can be pleaded for. They would raise mobs, for fear is very cruel. But the strong and healthy yeomen and husbands of the land, the self-sustaining class of inventive and industrious men, fear no competition or superiority. Come what will, their faculty cannot be spared.

The First of August marks the entrance of a new element into modern politics, namely, the civilization of the negro. A man is added to the human family. Not the least affecting part of this history of abolition, is, the annihilation of the old indecent nonsense about the nature of the negro. In the case of the ship Zong, in 1781, whose master had thrown one hundred and thirty-two slaves alive into the sea, to cheat the underwriters, the first jury gave a verdict in favor of the master and owners: they had a right to do what they had done. Lord Mansfield is reported to have said on the bench, "The matter left to the jury is,—Was it from necessity? For they had no doubt,— though it shocks one very much,—that the case of slaves was the same as if horses had been thrown overboard. It is a very shocking case. But a more enlightened and humane opinion began to prevail. Mr. Clarkson, early in his career, made a collection of African productions and manufactures as specimens of the arts and culture of the negro; comprising cloths and loom, weapons, polished stones and woods, leather, glass, dyes, ornaments, soap, pipe-bowls, and trinkets. These he showed to Mr. Pitt, who saw and handled them with extreme interest. On sight of these, says Clarkson, many sublime thoughts seemed to rush at once into his mind, some of which he expressed; and hence appeared to arise a project which was always dear to him, of the civilization of Africa,—a dream which forever elevates his fame. In 1791, Mr. Wilberforce announced to the House of Commons, We have already gained one victory we have obtained for these poor creatures the recognition of their human nature, which, for a time, was most shamefully denied them. It was the sarcasm of Montesquieu, "it would not do to suppose that negroes were men, lest it should turn out that whites were not;" for, the white has, for ages, done what he could to keep the negro in that hoggish state. His laws have been furies. It now appears, that the negro race is, more than any other, susceptible of rapid civilization. The emancipation is observed, in the islands, to have wrought for the negro a benefit as sudden as when a thermometer is brought out of the shade into the sun. It has given him eyes and ears. If, before, he was taxed with such stupidity, or such defective vision, that he could not set a table square to the walls of an apartment, he is now the principal, if not the only mechanic, in the West Indies; and is, besides, an architect, a physician, a lawyer, a magistrate, an editor, and a valued and increasing political power. The recent testimonies of Sturge, of Thome and Kimball, of Gurney, of Philippo, are very explicit on this point, the capacity and the success of the colored and the black population in employments of skill, of profit, and of trust; and, best of all, is the testimony to their moderation. They receive hints and advances from the whites, that they will be gladly received as subscribers to the Exchange, as members of this or that committee of trust. They hold back, and say to each other, that "social position is not to be gained by pushing."

I have said that this event interests us because it came mainly from the concession of the whites; I add, that in part it is the earning of the blacks. They won the pity and respect which they have received, by their powers and native endowments. I think this a circumstance of the highest import. Their whole future is in it. Our planet, before the age of written history, had its races of savages, like the generations of sour paste, or the animalcules that wriggle and bite in a drop of putrid water. Who cares for these or for their wars? We do not wish a world of bugs or of birds; neither afterward of Scythians,

Caraibs, or Feejees. The grand style of nature, her great periods, is all we observe in them. Who cares for oppressing whites, or oppressed blacks, twenty centuries ago, more than for bad dreams? Eaters and food are in the harmony of nature; and there too is the germ forever protected, unfolding gigantic leaf after leaf, a newer flower, a richer fruit, in every period, yet its next product is never to be guessed. It will only save what is worth saving; and it saves not by compassion, but by power. It appoints no police to guard the lion, but his teeth and claws; no fort or city for the bird, but his wings; no rescue for flies and mites, but their spawning numbers, which no ravages can overcome. It deals with men after the same manner. If they are rude and foolish, down they must go. When at last in a race, a new principle appears, an idea,—that conserves it; ideas only save races. If the black man is feeble, and not important to the existing races, not on a parity with the best race, the black man must serve, and be exterminated. But if the black man carries in his bosom an indispensable element of a new and coming civilization, for the sake of that element, no wrong, nor strength, nor circumstance, can hurt him: he will survive and play his part. So now, the arrival in the world of such men as Toussaint, and the Haytian heroes, or of the leaders of their race in Barbadoes and Jamaica, outweighs in good omen all the English and American humanity. The anti-slavery of the whole world, is dust in the balance before this,—is a poor squeamishness and nervousness: the might and the right are here: here is the anti-slave: here is man: and if you have man, black or white is an insignificance. The intellect,—that is miraculous! Who has it, has the talisman: his skin and bones, though they were of the color of night, are transparent, and the ever-lasting stars shine through, with attractive beams. But a compassion for that which is not and cannot be useful or lovely, is degrading and futile. All the songs, and news papers, and money-subscriptions, and vituperation of such as do not think with us, will avail nothing against a fact. I say to you, you must save yourself, black or white, man or woman; other help is none. I esteem the occasion of this jubilee to be the proud discovery, that the black race can contend with the white; that, in the great anthem which we call history, a piece of many parts and vast compass, after playing a long time a very low and subdued accompaniment, they perceive the time arrived when they can strike in with effect, and take a masters part in the music. The civility of the world has reached that pitch, that their more moral genius is becoming indispensable, and the quality of this race is to be honored for itself. For this, they have been preserved in sandy deserts, in rice-swamps, in kitchens and shoe-shops, so long: now let them emerge, clothed and in their own form.

There remains the very elevated consideration which the subject opens, but which belongs to more abstract views than we are now taking, this namely, that the civility of no race can be perfect whilst another race is degraded. It is a doctrine alike of the oldest, and of the newest philosophy, that, man is one, and that you cannot injure any member, without a sympathetic injury to all the members. America is not civil, whilst Africa is barbarous.

These considerations seem to leave no choice for the action of the intellect and the conscience of the country. There have been moments in this, as well as in every piece of moral history, when there seemed room for the infusions of a skeptical philosophy; when it seemed doubtful, whether brute force would not triumph in the eternal struggle. I doubt not, that sometimes a despairing negro, when jumping over the ships sides to escape from the white devils who surrounded him, has believed there was no vindication of right; it is horrible to think of, but it seemed so. I doubt not, that sometimes the negro's friend, in the face of scornful and brutal hundreds of traders and drivers, has felt his heart sink. Especially, it seems to me, some degree of despondency is pardonable, when he observes the men of conscience and of intellect, his own natural allies and champions,—those whose attention should be nailed to the grand objects of this cause, so hotly offended by whatever incidental petulances or infirmities of indiscreet defenders of the negro, as to permit themselves to be ranged with the enemies of the human race; and names which should be the alarums of liberty and the watchwords of truth, are mixed up with all the rotten rabble of selfishness and tyranny. I assure myself that this coldness and blindness will pass away. A single noble wind of sentiment will scatter them forever. I am sure that the good and wise elders, the ardent and generous youth will not permit what is incidental and exceptional to withdraw their devotion from the essential and permanent characters of the question. There have been moments, I said, when men might be forgiven, who doubted. Those moments are past. Seen in masses, it cannot be disputed, there is progress in human society. There is a blessed necessity by which the interest of men is always driving them to the right; and, again, making all crime mean and ugly. The genius of the Saxon race, friendly to liberty; the enterprise, the very muscular vigor of this nation, are inconsistent with slavery. The Intellect, with blazing eye, looking through history from the beginning onward, gazes on this blot, and it disappears. The sentiment of Right, once very low and indistinct, but ever more articulate, because it is the voice of the universe, pronounces Freedom. The Power that built this fabric of things affirms it in the heart; and in the history of the First of August, has made a sign to the ages, of his will.

# Bibliography

American Colonization Society, *The African Repository*, Vol. 49, p. 133.

Bouve, E. T., "Ancient Landmarks of Hingham Massachusetts," *History of Hingham*, 1894, p. 197.

Clark, A. J., "Hingham's Great Day," *Hingham Journal*, October 25, 1912.

Cornish, L. C., "A Seventeenth Century Cottage," *Good Housekeeping*, November 1904, pp. 517-21.

Dickerson, K., "Notes on Tranquility Lodge and Roseneath Cottage," 2018.

Douglass, F., *Autobiographies: Narrative of the Life, My Bondage and My Freedom, Life and Times*, Gates, H. L., (ed.), Library Classics of the United States, 1994.

Douglass, F., "West India Emancipation: Extract from a Speech in Elmira New York, 1 August 1880," appendix to *Life and Times of Frederick Douglass*, Gates, H. L., (ed.), Library Classics of the United States, 1994.

Douglass, F., *The Life and Times of Frederick Douglass*, 1892, Cosimo Classics, 2008, p. 341.

Ellis, H., (ed.), *The Reporter: Containing Decisions of the Supreme and Circuit Courts of the United States, Courts of Last Resort in the Several States, and of the English and Irish Courts, Volume 7*, Houghton Mifflin, Cambridge, The Riverside Press, 1879, p. 241.

Fearing, A., famousamerican.net/albertfearing.

Foner, E., *Gateway to Freedom: The Hidden History of the Underground Railroad*, W. W. Norton & Co., Inc., 2015.

Garrison, W. L., WGBH teacher resources: www.pbs.org/wgbh/aia/part4/4p1561.html.

Hart, L. L., and Hart, F. R., *Not All is Changed: A Life History of Hingham*, Hingham Historical Commission, 1993.

Hingham Historical Society, "Out of the Archives," 2014–2015, 2018. Tranquility Grove banners.

*Hingham Patriot*, various 1844 editions, Hingham Historical Society, Hingham Public Library.

Hingham, Town of, Conservation Commission, *Town of Hingham, Massachusetts Open Space and Recreation Plan*, Inventory of Lands of Conservation and Recreation Interest, 2009–2016.

Hutchinson, J. W., *Story of the Hutchinsons (Tribe of Jesse)*, Hutchinson, Lee and Shepard, Boston, 1896, pp. 120–122.

Massachusetts Historical Society, *The Diaries of John Quincy Adams, A Digital Collection*, July - September 1844.

Massachusetts Historical Society, Portraits of Abolitionist Figures, Images of the Anti-Slavery Movement in Massachusetts, and Online Resources.

Mehegan, D. J., "Albert Fearing's Dream," Hingham Public Library, September 20, 2012.

Papson, D., and Calarco, T., *Secret Lives of the Underground Railroad in New York City, Sydney Howard Gay, Louis Napoleon and the Record of Fugitives*, McFarland & Company, Inc., 2015.

Roberts, D., "Forgotten American Observance: Remembering the First of August," 23 pages. Recipient of 2001–2002 Sarah Ruth Award for best submission to Ex Post Facto.

Rugemer, E. B., *The Problem of Emancipation (Antislavery, Abolition and the Atlantic World)*, Louisiana State University Press, Kindle Edition, 2009.

Samuel J. May Anti-Slavery Collection, Cornell University Library, Division of Rare and Manuscript Collections, Ithaca, New York.

Sanborn, F. B., and Harris, W. T., "A. Bronson Alcott: His Life and Philosophy," Volume 1, Boston, Roberts Brothers, 1893, pp. 126–128.

Song of the Abolitionist, historyengine.richmond.edu/episodes/view/5565.

Soule, Richard, *Memorial of the Sprague family: a poem recited at a meeting in Duxbury of the descendants and connections of Hon. Seth Sprague, on the occasion of his 86th birthday, July 4, 1846*, James Munroe and Company, Boston, 1847.

Stearns, Rev. O., "The gospel applied to the fugitive slave law: A sermon preached to the Third Congregational Society of Hingham, On Sunday, March 2, 1851," W. Crosby and H. P. Nichols, Boston, 40 pages.

Stewart, J. B., *Wendell Phillips, Liberty's Hero*, Louisiana State University Press, 1986.

Studley, M. H., "An 'August First' in 1844," *The New England Quarterly, Inc.*, Vol. 16, No. 4, Boston, December 1943, pp. 567–577.

*The Liberator*, various 1844 and 1845 editions, including July 26, 1844, August 9, 1844.

Vinal, C., Hingham Conservation Commission, Hingham Conservation Land Trust Map, 1982.